Project English

アクティブに学ぶ英語コ

An Activity-based Guide to Everyday C　　　　c Grammar

Vivian Morooka
足立綾

NAN'UN-DO

このテキストの音声を無料で視聴（ストリーミング）・ダウンロードできます。自習用音声としてご活用ください。
以下のサイトにアクセスしてテキスト番号で検索してください。

https://nanun-do.com　テキスト番号［ **512131** ］

※ 無線 LAN（WiFi）に接続してのご利用を推奨いたします。

※ 音声ダウンロードは Zip ファイルでの提供になります。
　お使いの機器によっては別途ソフトウェア（アプリケーション）
　の導入が必要となります。

Project English 音声ダウンロードページは
左記の QR コードからもご利用になれます。

Read by
Shizuka Anderson
Chris Koprowski

Project English
An Activity-based Guide to Everyday Conversation and Basic Grammar
アクティブに学ぶ英語コミュニケーション

by
Vivian Morooka
Aya Adachi

Preface

PROJECT ENGLISH — An Activity-based Guide to Everyday Conversation and Basic Grammar is as the title describes: short, easy everyday conversations between an English-speaking classmate and a Japanese student to base the students' own conversations on; fill-in-the-blank listening activities to help the students improve their listening abilities; fun, interactive grammar-building activities; and an Active Learning section to reinforce what the students learned in each unit.

We wrote this book for Japanese beginning to intermediate English learners, to bridge the gap between high school and university-level English, and to fill in any gaps the students may have in their studies.

．．．

「プロジェクト・イングリッシュ」―この教科書は、タイトルどおり、日常英会話と基本的な英文法を学ぶためのアクティビティ・ベースの教科書です。学生たちが楽しみながら英語を学ぶことができるように、各項目にアクティブに取り組める工夫がなされています。

　各ユニットには、まず英語話者であるクラスメートと日本人学生の間で交わされる簡潔な日常英会話例があります。これらの会話例は、本教科書を使用する学生自身が英語で会話をしようとする際のよい模範となるでしょう。

　会話演習の後は、空欄を埋めながら行うリスニング演習、楽しくそしてインタラクティブな文法演習、そして学生が各ユニットで学んだことを強化するためのアクティブラーニング・セクションが続きます。

　この本は、日本人の初級から中級の英語学習者を対象に、大学レベルの英語に到達する前の「取りこぼし」をカバーし、スムースにその後の学習に進めることができるような学習内容となっています。このアクティビティ満載の教科書を楽しんでお使いいただければと思います。

Vivian Morooka
足立綾

Table of Contents

Page

Pre-Unit 6

Unit 1　Where are you from?
Subject-Verb Agreement　主語と動詞の一致 14

Unit 2　How are you doing?
Be Verbs & Do Verbs　Be 動詞と一般動詞 20

Unit 3　How many classes do you have?
Countable Nouns　数えられる名詞 28

Review 1 (Units 1-3) 33

Unit 4　How much food do you need for your party?
Uncountable Nouns　数えられない名詞 36

Unit 5　How many people are there in your family?
There is / There are / It is / They are
「ある」「いる」の表現と It is / They are との違い 42

Unit 6　When is your report due?
Cardinal & Ordinal Numbers　数 48

Review 2 (Units 4-6) 55

Unit 7　How was your weekend?
Past Tense　過去形 58

Unit 8　What time is your first class?
Time　時間の表現 64

Unit 9　Have you ever been to Kyoto?
Present Perfect　現在完了形 70

Review 3 (Units 7-9) 77

Unit 10　**Can I ask you a favor?**
　　　　　Auxiliary Verbs　助動詞 80

Unit 11　**I'm going to visit my grandparents.**
　　　　　Future Tense　未来形 86

Unit 12　**I'm on the train.**
　　　　　Prepositions　前置詞 92

Review 4 (Units 10-12) 99

Appendix
(Grammar Explanations in Japanese)
Units 1 – 12

0.　　Parts of Speech　品詞 102

1.　　Subject-Verb Agreement　主語と動詞の一致 104

2.　　Be Verbs & Do Verbs　Be 動詞と一般動詞 105

3 & 4. Countable & Uncountable Nouns　数えられる名詞と数えられない名詞 106

5.　　There is / There are / It is / They are 107
　　　　「ある」「いる」の表現と It is / They are との違い

6.　　Cardinal & Ordinal Numbers　数 109

7.　　Past Tense　過去形 111

8.　　Time　時間の表現 113

9.　　Present Perfect　現在完了形 114

10.　 Auxiliary Verbs　助動詞 115

11.　 Future Tense　未来形 116

12.　 Prepositions　前置詞 117

　ローマ字表記には、大きく分けて、ヘボン式と訓令式（日本式）の２種類があります。学校では訓令式を教えることもありますが、鉄道、道路標識、地名などにおいて実際に用いられることが多いのはヘボン式です。また、旅券（パスポート）の氏名表記は、原則として戸籍に記載された氏名について、ヘボン式ローマ字で表記することとされています（ヘボン式によらない表記の場合は申請が必要）。

　ここでは、訓令式とは異なる部分を確認しながら、ヘボン式ローマ字表記の決まりについて、見ていきましょう。

　There are mainly 2 methods to write Japanese in "Romaji" (the alphabet). Some schools teach the Kunrei method, which is favored by the Japanese government today, but the Hepburn method remains the world standard and is also used widely in Japan. You have to use the Hepburn method for names on passports. (You have to get special permission to write your name on your passport if it's not the Hepburn method.)

　Look at the chart, noting the difference between the Hepburn and Kunrei methods.

ヘボン式 Hepburn	訓令式 Kunrei	ヘボン式 Hepburn	訓令式 Kunrei	ヘボン式 Hepburn	訓令式 Kunrei
a i u e o ア イ ウ エ オ		ga gi gu ge go ガ ギ グ ゲ ゴ		kya kyu kyo キャ キュ キョ	
ka ki ku ke ko カ キ ク ケ コ		za ji zu ze zo ザ ジ ズ ゼ ゾ	zi ジ	sha shu sho シャ シュ ショ	sya syu syo シャ シュ ショ
sa shi su se so サ シ ス セ ソ	si シ	da ji zu de do ダ ヂ ヅ デ ド	di zi ヂ	cha chu cho チャ チュ チョ	tya tyu tyo チャ チュ チョ
ta chi tsu te to タ チ ツ テ ト		ba bi bu be bo バ ビ ブ ベ ボ		nya nyu nyo ニャ ニュ ニョ	
na ni nu ne no ナ ニ ヌ ネ ノ		pa pi pu pe po パ ピ プ ペ ポ		hya hyu hyo ヒャ ヒュ ヒョ	
ha hi fu he ho ハ ヒ フ ヘ ホ	hu フ			mya myu myo ミャ ミュ ミョ	zya zyu zyo ジャ ジュ ジョ
ma mi mu me mo マ ミ ム メ モ				rya ryu ryo リャ リュ リョ	
ya i yu e yo ヤ イ ユ エ ヨ				gya gyu gyo ギャ ギュ ギョ	
ra ri ru re ro ラ リ ル レ ロ				ja ju jo ジャ ジュ ジョ	
wa i u e o ワ イ ウ エ ヲ				bya byu byo ビャ ビュ ビョ	
n(m) ン				pya pyu pyo ピャ ピュ ピョ	

【注意するべき表記】Features:

- 撥音：B、M、P の前の「ん」は、N ではなく M で表記

  For "n" sounds before "b" "m" "p", use "m" not "n"

  例：難波（ナンバ）Namba、本間（ホンマ）Homma、晋平（シンペイ）Shimpei

  ※例外あり there are exceptions　例：群馬（グンマ）Gunma

  ただし、氏名表記の場合は上記に従う。

- 促音：子音を重ねて表記

  ※ただし、チ（chi）、チャ（cha）、チュ（chu）、チョ（cho）音の前には「t」を表記

  For doubled consonants, only the first consonant of the set is doubled, except for "ch", which is replaced by "tch".

  例 example：結果（ケッカ）kekka、ずっと zutto、一緒（イッショ）issho、三つ（ミッツ）mittsu、

  鳥取（トットリ）Tottori、堀田（ホッタ）Hotta、吉川（キッカワ）Kikkawa、ジャック Jakku

  例 example：抹茶 matcha（×maccha）、八丁（ハッチョウ）Hatcho（×Haccho）

- 長音の O や U は記入しない。ただし、末尾が「オオ」となる場合は OO と書く。

  The long vowel "o" and "u" are not written, except when the ending sound is the long vowel of "o".

  例 example：大阪（オオサカ）Osaka（×Oosaka）、大野（オオノ）Ono（×Oono）

  河野（コウノ）Kono（×Kouno）、洋子（ヨウコ）Yoko（×Youko）

  大河内（オオコウチ）Okochi（×Ookouchi）、光司（コウジ）Koji（×Kouji）

  翔子（ショウコ）Shoko（×Shouko）、次郎（ジロウ）Jiro（×Jirou）

  日向（ヒュウガ）Hyuga（×Hyuuga）、裕貴（ユウキ）Yuki（×Yuuki）

  優（ユウ）Yu（×Yuu）、伊藤（イトウ）Ito（×Itou）、高藤（タカトウ）Takato（×Takatou）

  妹尾（セノオ）Senoo（×Seno）、高遠（タカトオ）Takatoo（×Takato）

- 長音その他の例

  Some other rules for long vowels

  - 「ー」を省略する場合

    When the long vowel of "i" is written as "ー", "i" is not written.

    例 example：ニーナ（ニーナ）Nina、シーナ（シーナ）Shina、サリー（サリー）Sari

  - 「イ」を省略しない場合

    The combination of "i" + "i" is written "ii".

    例 example：新菜（ニイナ）Niina、しいな（シイナ）Shiina、さりい（サリイ）Sarii

Here are some expressions your teacher may say:
先生は下記のような表現を使います。

---

1. Please repeat (after me). （先生に続いて）くりかえしてください。

2. Please open your books. 本を開けてください。

3. Please close your books. 本を閉じてください。

4. Please look up and listen. 顔を上げて聞いてください。

5. Please clear your desks. 机の上を片付けてください。

6. Work in pairs. / Work in groups. ペア/グループになって行ってください。

7. Do Exercise 1 in class/for homework. 授業で/宿題で、問題1をやってください。

8. Please answer in a full sentence. 全文を使ってください。

9. Look at page ～. ～ページを見てください。

10. Exchange papers with a classmate. クラスメートとのプリントを交換してくだい。

11. Check your answers with a classmate. クラスメートと答え合わせをしてください。

12. Do you understand? わかりましたか？

Here are some questions/expressions you can use in class:
授業中、以下の表現を使って先生と話してみましょう。

---

1. May I ask a question? 質問してもよろしいでしょうか？

2. What does ～ mean? ～はどういう意味ですか？

3. Could you repeat that, please? すみません、もう1度言っていただけますか？

4. Pardon? もう1度言ってください。

5. How do you pronounce (say) this? これはどう発音しますか？

6. How do you spell ～? ～はどのようにつづりますか？

7. How do you say ～ in English? ～は英語でどのように言いますか？

8. What do you call this in English? これは英語でなんと言いますか？

9. What's the difference between ～ and ～? ～と～はどう違いますか？

10. May I go to the restroom? トイレへ行ってもよろしいですか？

11. I was absent/present last week. 私は先週、欠席/出席していました。

12. Yes, I understand. / Yes, I got it. はい、わかりました。

Walk around the room and ask your classmates these questions. When someone answers "Yes," ask him/her to sign on the line. The same person can sign only ONE time. 教室内を移動し、クラスメートに下にある質問をしましょう。答えが「Yes」だった場合は、下線部に名前を書いてもらいましょう。名前をかけるのは、1人につき1箇所のみです。いろいろなクラスメートと話しましょう。

Are you	an only child?	Yes, I am.	Can you	play tennis?	Yes, I can.
	on a diet?	No, I'm not.		ski?	No, I can't.
Do you	like natto?	Yes, I do.	Were you	born in the summer?	Yes, I was.
	have a pet?	No, I don't.		at home yesterday?	No, I wasn't.

1. Are you an only child?

2. Were you born in the summer?

3. Do you like spaghetti?

4. Can you ski?

5. Do you have two brothers?

6. Can you play the piano?

7. Do you like to study?

8. Do you like rock music?

9. Are you hungry?

10. Are you on a diet?

11. Do you come from a big city?

12. Do you have a dog?

13. Do you like English?

14. Are you a good swimmer?

15. Do you get up early?

Use these expressions:

"May I ask you a question?"   "Sure."
"Please sign here."   "OK."
(After "No, I ...") "Thanks, anyway." / "That's OK."

1. Argentina
2. Australia
3. Austria
4. Brazil
5. Canada

6. China
7. the Czech Republic
8. Egypt
9. Finland
10. France

11. Germany
12. India
13. Italy
14. Japan
15. Kenya

16. Mexico
17. Mongolia
18. New Zealand
19. the Philippines
20. Russia

21. Saudi Arabia
22. South Africa
23. South Korea
24. Spain
25. Sweden

26. Thailand
27. Turkey
28. the UK (the United Kingdom)
29. the USA (the United States of America)
30. Vietnam

Project English

An Activity-based Guide to Everyday Conversation and Basic Grammar

アクティブに学ぶ英語コミュニケーション

Vivian Morooka

Aya Adachi

南雲堂
NAN'UN-DO

ASAKUSA

SKY TREE

Today's Lunch

Chiken Salad

Unit 1

Where are you from?

Subject-Verb Agreement

I. Conversation 1

As you listen to the conversation below, fill in the missing parts. Check your answers with a partner and your teacher. Repeat each line after your teacher, and then take turns practicing the conversation with your partner, changing roles each time. 会話を聞き、下の会話文の下線部を埋めましょう。パートナーと答えを確認してください。そのあと、先生と答え合わせをし、先生に続いて文を復唱してください。最後にパートナーと会話を練習しましょう。1度読み終えたら次は役を交代してもう1度行いましょう。

Ayaka and John are classmates. On the first day of classes, Ayaka greets John before class begins. アヤカとジョンはクラスメートです。最初の授業が始まる前に、アヤカがジョンに挨拶しています。 🎧02

Ayaka: Hello.

John: (1)_____.

Ayaka: My name's Ayaka.

John: (2)_____ John.

Ayaka: (3)_____ are you (4)_____, John?

John: I'm from (5)_____ _____.

Ayaka: So, you're (6)_____. I'm Japanese. I (7)_____ _____ Mito, Ibaraki.

John: Oh, the (8)_____ here. Let's talk (9)_____.

Questions: Work with a partner. Take turns asking and answering the questions below about **Conversation 1**. Answer **in full sentences,** and write the answers on the lines using the correct pronouns (He/She/His/Her/It). ペアで行います。Conversation 1 の会話について、下の質問をし、答えを書き取りましょう。答えるときは、単語ではなく文章（主語・述語がはいった文）で答えること。1 人だけが聞いたり 1 人だけが答えたりするのではなく、交互に質問し、2 人とも全ての質問をし、全ての質問に答えるようにすること。

1. What's her name? _____

2. What's his name? _____

3. Where is he from? _____

4. Where does she come from? _____

5. What's his nationality*? _____

Practice: With a partner, write a conversation based on **Conversation 1**. Fill in the blanks below with information about yourselves. Take turns reading your conversation out loud, changing roles each time. パートナーと協力して空欄を埋め、自分たちに関するオリジナル会話文を作りましょう。書き終えたら声に出して 2 度練習します。大きくはっきりとした声で読み上げること。2 度目は役を交代して読み上げましょう。

A: Hello.

B: _____.

A: My name's _____.

B: I'm _____.

A: Where are you from, _____[name]?

B: I'm from _____[city], _____[Prefecture*]. And you?

A: I come from _____[city], _____[Prefecture].

* nationality 国籍　prefecture 県

15

II. Grammar & Practice: Countries, Nationalities and Languages

Exercise 1: Work in a group. Take turns reading each line below. Fill in the blanks with the missing country, nationality, or language. Try to do all 13 before looking at a dictionary.　グループで行います。下の表の国名、国籍名、言語名を交代で読み上げながら空欄に適切な国名、国籍名、言語名を入れていきましょう。まずは辞書を使わずにすべて埋められるよう協力して行いましょう。

Example:　The country is **Japan.**　The people are **Japanese.**　They speak **Japanese.**

	Country	Nationality	Language
1	the USA (the United States of America)	American	
2		Vietnamese	
3	Australia		
4		Austrian	
5		Thai	
6		Brazilian	
7	Mexico		
8		Filipino	Tagalog/English
9	India		
10		Spanish	
11	France		French
12		German	
13	the UK (the United Kingdom)		

Exercise 2: Work together in a group. Look at the map in the Pre-Unit and choose five other countries. On the lines below, write the names of the countries, the people's nationality, and the language(s) they speak.　グループで協力して行います。Pre Unit D の世界地図を見て上の表にはない国を5つ選び、国名、国籍名、言語名を下線部に書きこみましょう。

	Country	Nationality	Language
1.	_____	_____	_____
2.	_____	_____	_____
3.	_____	_____	_____
4.	_____	_____	_____
5.	_____	_____	_____

III. Conversation 2

Listen to the conversation below. Then take turns practicing it with a partner, changing roles each time.
会話を聞き、パートナーと一緒に練習しましょう。1 度読み終えたら役を交代してもう 1 度練習します。

Ayaka and John talk after class.   アヤカとジョンは授業の後に話をしています。   03

John: Good class!

Ayaka: I think so, too.

John: Well, I have to go to my next class.

Ayaka: Me, too. What's your next class?

John: Biology*. And yours?

Ayaka: Chemistry*.

John: Nice meeting you, Ayaka.

Ayaka: Nice meeting you, too, John.

John: See you next week, then.

Ayaka: Right. Bye, John.   * Biology 生物学   Chemistry 化学

Practice: With a partner, write a conversation based on **Conversation 2**. Fill in the blanks below with information about yourselves. Take turns reading your conversation out loud, changing roles each time.
パートナーと協力し、上の Conversation 2 をもとに、自分たちに関するオリジナル会話文を作成しましょう。書き終えたら声に出して 2 度練習します。大きくはっきりとした声で読み上げること。2 度目は役を交代して読み上げましょう。

A: _____ class!

B: I think so, too.

A: Well, I _____.

B: _____. What _____?

A: _____. _____?

B: _____.

A: Nice meeting you, _____.

B: _____, _____.

A: See you _____, then.

B: Right. Bye, _____.

IV. Active Learning

Read the Grammar section on Subject-Verb Agreement in the **Appendix** on page 104 (Unit 1 Subject-Verb Agreement). Then look at the pronouns and verb forms in the box below.　付録104 ページの「主語と動詞の一致」の説明と下の表をよく読みましょう。

Singular（単数）:

I **am/speak/do**

You **are/speak/do**

He/She/It **is/speaks/does**

Plural（複数）:

We **are/speak/do**

You **are/speak/do** (2 or more people)

They **are/speak/do** (2 or more people/things)

Spelling: (verbs after **He/She/It**)

-s   buys, thinks, comes, plays, takes, has, rides

-es   (after: ch, o, s, sh, x, z) catches, washes, goes, misses, passes

-ies   (after: consonant［子音］＋y) studies, cries, tries

Every and each use 3rd-person singular.

Everyone is …

Everybody gets …

Each person wins …

Everything does …

A person (1)

People (2+)

Exercise 1: Fill in the blank in each sentence below with the correct form of the appropriate verb. 適切な動詞と動詞の形を用いて 1 ～ 10 の空欄を埋めましょう。

1. A person from Germany _____ German.

2. People from the U.K. _____ British.

3. _____ French people from France?

4. _____ she from India?

5. Ayaka _____ English at this school.

6. John and Mary _____ from the U.S.

7. Everyone here _____ the tests.

8. Mary _____ an older brother.

9. Brian _____ to school on foot.

10. Mary and I _____ bikes to school.

Exercise 2: With a partner, take turns asking and answering the questions below. Write your partner's answers **in full sentences**, using the correct pronouns (**He/She/They/It**) and verb forms. パートナーに下記の質問をしましょう。質問ごとに交互に聞き合います。相手の答えを文章で書き込んでください。適切な代名詞と動詞の形を用いること。

1. Where do you come from?

   _____

2. Where does your mother or father come from?

   _____

3. Where do you live?

   _____

4. Where do your parents live?

   _____

5. What do you usually do after this class?

   _____

6. What does your best friend do?

   _____

7. How do you come to school?

   _____

8. How long does it take you to get to school?

   _____

9. What food do you like best?

   _____ best.

10. What do you usually eat/have for lunch?

    _____

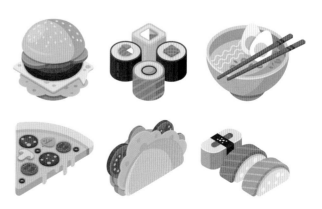

How are you doing?

Be Verbs & Do Verbs

Mito   San Francisco

I. Conversation 1

As you listen to the conversation below, fill in the missing parts. Check your answers with a partner and with your teacher. Repeat each line after your teacher, and then take turns practicing the conversation with your partner, changing roles each time.　会話を聞き、下の会話文の下線部を埋めましょう。パートナーと答えを確認してください。そのあと、先生と答え合わせをし、先生に続いて文を復唱してください。最後にパートナーと会話を練習しましょう。1度読み終えたら次は役を交代してもう1度行いましょう。

Ayaka and John talk just before class begins.　授業の前に、アヤカとジョンがまた話をしています。　🎧04

Ayaka: Hi, John. How are you?

John: (1)_____! How are you (2)_____?

Ayaka: I'm fine. By the way, what's your (3)_____ name, John?

John: It's (4)_____. What's yours?

Ayaka: My (5)_____ _____ is Nakayama.

John: Where do you (6)_____, Ayaka?

Ayaka: Right now, I (7)_____ _____ Narita, Chiba Prefecture, but I come from

Mito, Ibaraki. What (8)_____ are you from?

John: (9)_____ _____ San Francisco, California.

Ayaka: Let's talk (10)_____ class.

John: OK.

Questions: Work with a partner. Take turns asking and answering the questions below about **Conversation 1**. Answer **in full sentences** and write the answers on the lines using the appropriate pronouns. ペアで行います。Conversation 1 の会話について、パートナーに下の質問をし、答えを書き取りましょう。答えるときは、単語ではなく文章（主語・述語がはいった文）で答えること。1 人だけが聞いたり 1 人だけが答えたりするのではなく、交互に質問し、2 人とも全ての質問をし、全ての質問に答えるようにすること。

1. How is John doing? _____

2. What's John's last name? _____

3. What's Ayaka's last name? _____

4. Where does Ayaka live? _____

5. Where does John come from? _____

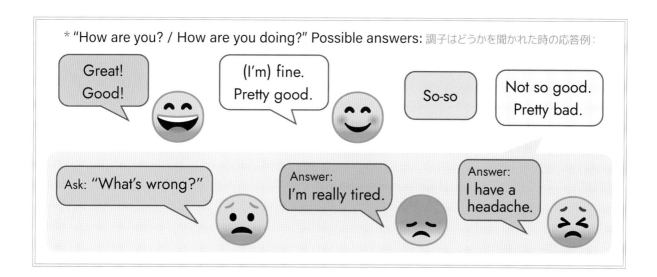

Practice: With a partner, write a conversation based on **Conversation 1**. Fill in the blanks below with information about yourselves. Take turns reading your conversation out loud, changing roles each time. パートナーと協力して空欄を埋め、自分たちに関するオリジナル会話文を作りましょう。書き終えたら声に出して 2 度練習します。大きくはっきりとした声で読み上げること。2 度目は役を交代して読み上げましょう。

A: Hi, _____. How are you?

B: _____. How are you doing?

A: _____. By the way, what's your last name?

B: It's _____. What's yours?

A: It's _____. Where do you live?

B: Right now, I live in _____, _____, (but) I come from _____, _____. And you?

A: I live in _____, _____. (But) I come from _____,

_____.

II. Grammar & Practice: Be and Do verbs   Be 動詞と一般動詞

Verbs are either "**Be**" or "**Do**" verbs. Read the **Appendix** on page 105 (Unit 2 Be Verbs & Do Verbs) and look at the chart below.
動詞には、Be 動詞と一般動詞があります。付録 105 ページの「Be 動詞と一般動詞」の説明と下の表の説明をよく読みましょう。

"**Be**" verbs:		"**Do**" verbs:
I am/was	We are/were	like, live, do, have, work, ...
You are/were	You (2+) are/were	(all other verbs)
He/She/It is/was	They are/were	

All "**Do**" verbs have "**do**" inside them: Like = **do like** の意味; live = **do live** の意味, etc.

The "**do**" comes out when we make **questions**: **Do** you **like** dogs? **Does** he **live** here?

And when we use the **negative** (**not**) form, "**not**" comes after "**do**" and often shortened: I **don't like** dogs. He **doesn't live** here.

Exercise 1: Work with a partner and fill in the blanks in the sentences below with the appropriate form of "Be" or "Do" verbs.   パートナーと協力し、Be 動詞または一般動詞を適切な形にして下記の 1 〜 12 の空欄を埋め、各文章を完成させましょう。

1. What animal _____ you like best?

2. _____ you watch TV often?

3. What _____ your father (or mother) do?

4. _____ your mother a housewife?

5. How many people _____ (there) in your family?

6. When _____ your birthday?

7. How many classes _____ you have today?

8. _____ your school near your house?

9. _____ you and your parents live in the same town?

10. How many brothers and sisters _____ you have?

11. _____ your father (or mother) work in an office?

12. _____ you and your best friend in the same class?

Exercise 2: With a partner, take turns asking and answering the questions above. Write your partner's answers **in full sentences**. Make sure you use the correct "Be" or "Do" verb forms and pronouns.   パートナーに上記の質問をしましょう。質問ごとに交互に聞き合います。相手の答えを文章で書き込んでください。Be 動詞、一般動詞のどちらが入るかを考え、適切な形にして正しい代名詞を用いてください。

1. _____

2. _____

3. _____

4. _____

5. _____

6. _____

7. _____

8. _____

9. _____

10. _____

11. _____

12. _____

III. Conversation 2

Listen to the conversation below. Then take turns practicing it with a partner, changing roles each time.
会話を聞き、パートナーと一緒に練習しましょう。１度読み終えたら役を交代してもう１度練習します。

Ayaka and John talk after class again.　アヤカとジョンは授業の後にまた話をしています。　🎧05

　　　Ayaka: What's your major, John?

　　　John:　I'm a Japanese history major. What's yours?

　　　Ayaka: My major is teaching. I want to be a Japanese teacher in the Philippines.
　　　　　　 What about you?

　　　John:　I want to work at a museum in Japan, if possible.

　　　Ayaka: Why do you want to work in Japan?

　　　John:　I love Japan!

Practice: With a partner, write a conversation based on **Conversation 2**. Fill in the blanks below with information about yourselves. Take turns reading your conversation out loud, changing roles each time.
パートナーと協力し、上の Conversation 2 をもとに、自分たちに関するオリジナル会話文を作成しましょう。書き終えたら声に出して２度練習します。大きくはっきりとした声で読み上げること。２度目は役を交代して読み上げましょう。

A: What's your major, _____?

B: I'm a(n) _____ major. What's yours?

A: My major is _____. I want to be a(n) _____. What about you?

B: I want to be a(n) _____. Why do you want to be a(n) _____?

A: _____. And you? Why do you want to be a

　 _____?

B: _____.

IV. Active Learning

Exercise 1: Work with a partner. Using the hints in the parentheses below, write questions to ask each other. Go over the questions with your teacher. Then take turns asking and answering the questions with your partner. Write your partner's answers on the lines **in full sentences**. Make sure you use the correct pronouns and verb forms. （　　　）内のヒントを参考に、パートナーに対する質問を考えて下線部に書き込みましょう。先生に確認してもらった後、パートナーと質疑応答の練習をしましょう。主語と述語動詞を含む文章で聞き、同じく文章で答えること。聞き取った相手の答えを下線部に文章ごと書き入れてください。適切な動詞と形、正しい代名詞を用いること。

1. (first name)

   _____ ?

   Partner's answer: _____

2. (last name)

   _____ ?

   Partner's answer: _____

3. (live)

   _____ ?

   Partner's answer: _____

4. (from)

   _____ ?

   Partner's answer: _____

5. (major)

   _____ ?

   Partner's answer: _____

6. (do free time)

   _____ ?

   Partner's answer: _____

7. (old)

   _____ ?

   Partner's answer: _____

8. (birthday)

   _____ ?

   Partner's answer: _____

9. (How come to school)

    _____?

    Partner's answer: _____

10. (How many ... family)

    _____?

    Partner's answer: _____

11. (own question)

    _____?

    Partner's answer: _____

12. (own question)

    _____?

    Partner's answer: _____

Exercise 2: Working with another pair, introduce your partner to the others. To make your sentences, use the hints in TOPICS below and the information you learned about your partner in **Active Learning**, **Exercise 1**. Start your introduction as in the Example below. As you listen to the others, fill in the blanks in My Group with the appropriate information.

Example 例： "I would like to introduce you to Junko Watanabe. She lives in ... now, (but) she comes from ..."

TOPICS

	1, 2. First Name Last Name	3, 4. Lives now / Hometown	5. Major	6. Free time
MY GROUP				
My partner:				
Other pair (1):				
Other pair (2):				
Myself:				

もう１組のペアと一緒に行います。あなたのパートナーを他のふたりに紹介しましょう。TOPICS にあるヒントと Active Learning Exercise 1 で得たパートナーの情報を用いて文章にします。左ページの例を参考に始めてください。他の人が話している時には、内容を聞き取り、MY GROUP の適切な箇所に書き込みましょう。

TOPICS

7. Age	8. Birthday	9. How come to school	10. People in family	11, 12. Extra information
MY GROUP				

Unit 3

How many classes do you have?

Countable Nouns

I. Conversation 1

As you listen to the conversation below, fill in the missing parts. Check your answers with a partner and with your teacher. Repeat each line after your teacher, and then take turns practicing the conversation with your partner, changing roles each time. 会話を聞き、下の会話文の下線部を埋めましょう。パートナーと答えを確認してください。そのあと、先生と答え合わせをし、先生に続いて文を復唱してください。最後にパートナーと会話を練習しましょう。1度読み終えたら次は役を交代してもう1度行いましょう。

Ayaka and John talk before class begins. 授業が始まる前に、アヤカとジョンが話しています。 🎧06

Ayaka: You have (1)_____ _____ _____ books, John.

John: I know! I have (2)_____ classes. Don't you?

Ayaka: Well, I have only a couple of* classes today, so I (3)_____ _____ many

books. And (4)_____ instructors* use handouts*. Today's (5)_____

_____ _____ .

John: These books are big and (6)_____ . My back hurts*. (7)_____ _____

classes do you have tomorrow?

Ayaka: I have only (8)_____ classes tomorrow, too.

John: Good for you!

Ayaka: Yeah, but I have (9)_____ assignment* to do tonight, for my anthropology* class.

John: Oh, what do you have to do?

Ayaka: I have to read (10)_____ _____ and prepare for a presentation.

＊a couple of 2〜3の　instructor 講師　handout プリント　hurt 痛い　assignment 課題　anthropology 人類学

Questions: Work with a partner. Take turns asking and answering the questions below about **Conversation 1**. Answer **in full sentences** and write the answers on the lines using the appropriate pronouns (He/She/They). パートナーと行いましょう。Conversation 1 の会話について、下の質問をし、答えを書き取りましょう。答えるときは、単語ではなく文章（主語・述語がはいった文）で答えること。1 人だけが聞いたり 1 人だけが答えたりするのではなく、交互に質問し、2 人とも全ての質問をし、全ての質問に答えるようにすること。

1. Why does John have a lot of books? _____

2. Why doesn't Ayaka have many books today?

    _____

3. What are John's books like*? _____

4. How many classes does Ayaka have tomorrow?

    _____

5. What does Ayaka have to do for homework?

    _____

*What … like? どんな様に

Practice: With a partner, write a conversation based on **Conversation 1**. Fill in the blanks below with information about yourselves. Take turns reading your conversation out loud, changing roles each time. パートナーと協力して空欄を埋め、自分たちに関するオリジナル会話文を作りましょう。書き終えたら声に出して 2 度練習します。大きくはっきりとした声で読み上げること。2 度目は役を交代して読み上げましょう。

A: You have _____. Why?

B: I _____. Don't you?

A: I _____.

B: How many _____?

A: I _____. Today's _____.

B: _____.

A: I also have _____.

B: What do you have to do?

A: I have to _____.

II. Grammar & Practice: Regular plurals of nouns

Read the **Appendix** on page 106 (Unit 3&4 Countable & Uncountable Nouns) and the explanation below about how to form the regular plurals of nouns. 付録 106 ページの「数えられる名詞と数えられない名詞」の説明と下の表の説明をよく読み、名詞の複数形（規則的に変化するもの）について確認してください。

1. Add –**s** to regular nouns: a book—**books**, an instructor—**instructors**, a cake—**cakes**

2. If a word ends in –**s**, –**ss**, –**ch**, –**sh**, –**x**, or –**z**, add –**es**: a bus—**buses**, a dress—**dresses**, a watch—**watches**, a dish—**dishes**, a box—**boxes**, a waltz—**waltzes**

3. Double –z before adding –es: **quizzes**

4. Usually change –**f or –fe** to –**ves**: a wife—**wives**, a calf*—**calves** (except: a chef—**chefs**, a roof*—**roofs**, and some others)

5. **Change –y to –i and add –es**, except for words with vowels before the –y: a city—**cities**, a cherry—**cherries** (but, a boy—**boys**, a monkey—**monkeys**)

6. Add –**es** to words ending in –**o**: a potato—**potatoes**, a tomato—**tomatoes** (except: a photo—**photos**, a piano—**pianos**, and some others)

7. There are many **irregular*** plurals of nouns: a child—**children**, a man—**men**, a woman—**women**, a tooth—**teeth**, a foot—**feet**

8. Some nouns don't change the form for singular and plural: a fish—two **fish**, a sheep—many **sheep**

* calf 子牛　roof 屋根　irregular 不規則な

Exercise 1: Work with a partner. Take turns saying and writing the plurals of the nouns below. ペアで行います。1 ～ 12 までの名詞の複数形を言い、下線部に書き込みましょう。

1. a wish _____
2. a knife _____
3. a cat _____
4. an apple _____
5. a volcano* _____
6. a/the library _____

7. a fish _____
8. a French fry _____
9. a man _____
10. a woman _____
11. a person _____
12. a/the coach _____

* volcano 火山

Exercise 2: Work with a partner. On the lines below, write the correct form—singular or plural—of the nouns in parentheses. ペアで行います。1 ～ 10 までの（　　）内の名詞を単数形もしくは複数形にして下線部に書きましょう。

1. I put all of my _____(paper) from class in my backpack.

2. Add four _____(potato) to the curry.

3. That _____(children) was very quiet at school today.

4. I have a few* _____(pencil) in my pencil case.

5. Many _____(orange) are on the tree.

6. A _____(women) I know works at that convenience store.

7. I love _____(strawberry).

8. He used two _____(match) to light the candle.

9. After Susan ran three kilometers, both of her _____(foot) hurt.

10. Mari has two _____(boss) at her part-time job.

* a few 少し

III. Conversation 2

Read and listen to the conversation below. Then take turns practicing it with a partner, changing roles each time. 会話を聞き、パートナーと一緒に練習しましょう。1度読み終えたら役を交代してもう1度練習します。

Ayaka and John talk after class. アヤカとジョンが授業の後に話をしています。   🎧07

    Ayaka: Where are you going after school today?

    John:　I'm going to the mall.

    Ayaka: What will you do there?

    John:　I'll eat at the food court.

    Ayaka: What are you having for dinner?

    John:　I'll have a hamburger and some French fries.

    Ayaka: That sounds good.

    John:　What are you having for dinner?

    Ayaka: I think I'll eat a couple of rice balls. I'm on a diet.

    John:　Really? I should go on a diet, too.

Practice: With a partner, write a conversation based on **Conversation 2**. Fill in the blanks below with information about yourselves. Take turns reading your conversation out loud, changing roles each time.
パートナーと協力し、上の Conversation 2 をもとに、自分たちに関するオリジナル会話文を作成しましょう。書き終えたら声に出して2度練習します。大きくはっきりとした声で読み上げること。2度目は役を交代して読み上げましょう。

A: Where are you going after school today?

B: I'm _____.

A: What are you doing there?

B: I'm _____.

A: What are you having for dinner?

B: I'll have _____.

A: That sounds good.

B: What are you having for dinner?

A: I think I'll have _____.

B: Really? I think I will _____.

IV. Active Learning

Work with a partner. Fill in the blank in each question below with the correct form of the noun in parentheses. Then ask your partner the questions. Write your partner's answers on the lines in complete sentences. ペアで行います。名詞を適切な形にして下線部を埋め1〜10の文章を完成させましょう。終わったらパートナーに1〜10を聞きましょう。各質問の下の下線部にパートナーの答えを文章にして書き込みましょう。ピリオドも忘れずに。

1. How many _____(child) do your parents have?

   _____

2. How many _____(egg) are in your refrigerator*?

   _____

3. Do you have any _____(tissue) in your bag?

   _____

4. Do you like _____(cherry)?

   _____

5. How many _____(class) do you have (in) a week?

   _____

6. Do you have many _____(knife), _____(spoon), and _____(fork) in your drawer*?

   _____

7. How many _____(photo) are on your cellphone?

   _____

8. How many _____(man) and how many _____(woman) are in this classroom?

   _____

9. Are there any _____(convenience store) near here?

   _____

10. How many _____(tooth) do most adults have?

    _____

* refrigerator 冷蔵庫　drawer 引出し

● **Review Game**

Work with a group, but use only one book. Follow these instructions:
下記の 1 ～ 4 の指示に従い、グループで行います。教科書は 1 冊だけ使って構いません。（コインが必要です）

1.   Use a small object such as an eraser or a piece of paper as a marker.
     消しゴムや付箋のような小さなものを 1 つ用意してください。駒として使います。

2.   Play "rock, paper, scissors" to decide who goes first. Take turns moving your marker.
     ジャンケンをして順番を決めます。表の 1 から順に交代で進めます。

3.   Each player takes a turn by flipping a coin. If the coin lands face up, move two spaces. If the coin
     lands tails up, move one space.
     各プレイヤーが交代でコインを投げます。コインが表の場合は 2 つ進めてください。コインが裏の場合は 1 つしか進めません。

4.   When you land on a space, ask and answer the question on it. Answer **in a full sentence**.
     とまったマスの質問を読み上げて、正しい英文で答えましょう。

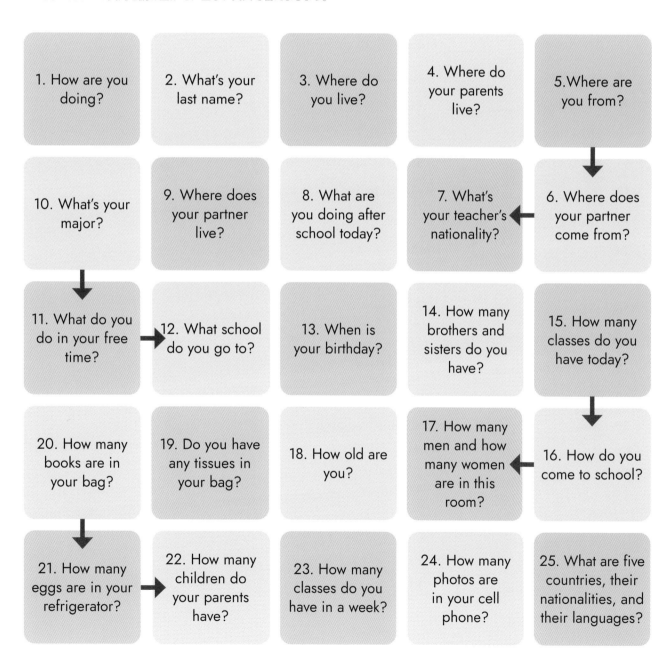

Part A: Work with a partner. As you take turns reading the sentences below, fill in the blanks with the most appropriate word or words.　ペアで行います。1～20 の空欄に入る適切な語を考え、文章を交代で読み上げていきます。各文ごとに空欄を埋めていきます。

1. People from the UK are _____ citizens*.

2. What _____ your favorite kind of* music?

3. _____ John and Aya take the same class?

4. _____ your best friend a student, too?

5. _____ your school near your house?

6. What _____ your father do?

7. My sister _____ a high school student.

8. How many classes _____ you have today?

9. I like dogs. _____ very friendly!

10. How many pets _____ Mayu have?

11. Many chairs _____ in this classroom.

12. _____ you and your parents live in the same town?

13. How _____ Akihiro come to school?

14. _____ you have a pet?

15. _____ he like strawberries?

16. When _____ your birthday?

17. How many computers _____ in this room?

18. What school _____ you go to?

19. _____ those students from the Philippines?

20. Robert _____ sports in his free time.

* citizen 国民　kind of 種類の

Part B: Work with a partner. On the lines, write the correct form—singular or plural—of the nouns in parentheses. ペアで行います。（　　　）内の名詞を単数形または複数形の正しい形にして下線部に書き込みましょう。

1. The server put two _____(dish) on the table.

2. Slice all of the _____(tomato) for our salad, please.

3. The sushi chef has six different _____(knife).

4. How many _____(quiz) do we have in this class?

5. Many _____(boy) are climbing that tree.

6. Two _____(man) are cleaning all the _____(window) in the school.

7. Of all fruit, I like _____ (cherry) best.

8. I went fishing and caught two _____(fish).

9. How many _____(tooth) do sharks have?

10. I am an only _____(children). I don't have any _____(brother) or
    _____(sister).

Unit 4

How much food do you need for your party?

Uncountable nouns

milk
eggs
cheese
meat
cola
fruit
rice
orange juice

I. Conversation 1

As you listen to the conversation below, fill in the missing parts. Check your answers with a partner and with your teacher. Repeat each line after your teacher, and then take turns practicing the conversation with your partner, changing roles each time.　会話を聞き、下の会話文の下線部を埋めましょう。パートナーと答えを確認してください。そのあと、先生と答え合わせをし、先生に続いて文を復唱してください。最後にパートナーと会話を練習しましょう。1度読み終えたら次は役を交代してもう1度行いましょう。

Ayaka and John meet each other by accident at a supermarket near their school.
アヤカとジョンは大学近くのスーパーで会いました。　　　　　　　　　　🎧08

John:　Hi, Ayaka. Nice to see you. What are you shopping for?

Ayaka:　Oh, hello, John! I'm getting (1)_____ food for a friend's birthday party tomorrow night. What about you?

John:　I'm buying food for the week.

Ayaka:　What do you usually buy?

John:　I usually buy (2)_____ _____ _____ milk, (3)_____ _____ _____ eggs, (4)_____ cheese, fruit, meat, and rice. What are you having at your party?

Ayaka:　We're having (5)_____ cake and some pizzas.

John:　That sounds* good. What are you getting to drink?

Ayaka:　I'm getting (6)_____ _____ _____ cola, and some orange juice, and several cans of green tea.

John:　(7)_____ _____ pizzas are you getting?

Ayaka: I think we'll need (8)_____ pizzas. Oh, I should get some salad, too.

John: I don't really like (9)_____, but I love pizza.

Ayaka: (10)_____ _____ like to come to the party?

John: Sure. I'm free* tomorrow night.

* sound(s) と思う   free 空いている

Questions: Work with a partner. Take turns asking and answering the questions about **Conversation 1**. Answer **in full sentences** and write the answers on the lines using the appropriate pronouns and verb forms.   ペアで行います。Conversation 1 の会話について、下の質問をし、答えを書き取りましょう。答えるときは、適切な代名詞と適切な動詞の形を用いて、単語ではなく文章（主語・述語がはいった文）で答えること。1 人だけが聞いたり 1 人だけが答えたりするのではなく、交互に質問し、2 人とも全ての質問をし、全ての質問に答えるようにすること。

1. What is Ayaka shopping for?

    _____

2. What is John shopping for?

    _____

3. What food does John usually buy for a week?

    _____

4. How much food is Ayaka getting for her party?

    _____

5. How many drinks is she getting?

    _____

Practice: With a partner, write a conversation based on **Conversation 1**. Fill in the blanks below with information about yourselves. Take turns reading your conversation out loud, changing roles each time.   パートナーと協力して空欄を埋め、自分たちに関するオリジナル会話文を作りましょう。書き終えたら声に出して 2 度練習します。大きくはっきりとした声で読み上げること。2 度目は役を交代して読み上げましょう。

A: Hi, _____. What are you shopping for?

B: I'm getting _____ for _____. What about you?

A: I'm buying _____.

B: _____?

A: I _____.

B: That sounds _____. I'm getting _____

    _____.

A: That sounds _____. What are you getting to _____?

B: I'm buying _____.

A: I _____(like/don't really like) _____.

II. Grammar & Practice: Countable and Uncountable nouns

Some nouns (car, book, tree) are countable. This means we can count them with numbers. Most countable nouns stand for things with a set shape. Other nouns (water, rice, sleep, advice) are uncountable, which means we cannot count them with numbers. And some nouns (glass/glasses, time/times) are both countable and uncountable. Read the **Appendix** on page 106 (Units 3 & 4 Countable & Uncountable Nouns).　名詞には数えられるものと数えられないものがあります。数えられるとはつまり数を使って人やモノについて言えるということです。例えば車1台、本3冊、4本の木といったように、数えられるものには、大抵形があります。数えられない名詞というのは、例えば液体、またお米などの小さく通常1つ1つ数えないもの、睡眠、助言などで数を使って数えられないもの・ことを指します。ただし、同じ名詞でも数えられる場合と数えられない場合があるものもあります（例えば glass/glasses, time/times などです）。付録106ページの「数えられる名詞と数えられない名詞」をもう1度よく読み、下記の表を参照してください。

Countable nouns　数えられる名詞	Uncountable nouns　数えられない名詞
1. Things we can count: "1 thing, 2, 3 …**s**"	1. Things we can't count: things that are **liquid, too small, can't be touched, collective (group).**
2. Can be plural (**−s or irregular plurals**)	
3. "**How many …s?**"	2. Usually can't be plural (usually no **−s**)
4. "**not many …s**"	3. "**How much …?**"
5. "**not any …s**"	4. "**not much …**"
6. "**There are …s.**"	5. "**not any …**"
7. "**a lot of …s**"	6. "**There is …**"
8. "**a few …s**"	7. "**a lot of …**"
9. "**a …/some …s**"	8. "**a little …**"
10. "**I like …s.**"	9. "**some …**"
	10. "**I like …**"

Exercise 1: First, repeat the words in the list below after your teacher. Next, with a partner, decide whether each word is Countable, Uncountable, or Both and write the word in the proper place below. **Write the plural forms of the countable nouns.** Then take turns pronouncing all the words you have written.　まず、下の青い四角の中の単語を先生の後について発音してください。次にどの名詞が数えられるか、または数えられないか、あるいは数えたり数えなかったりするかをパートナーと話し合い、下のリストに振り分けて書き入れてください。**数えられる名詞については、複数形にして書いてください。**最後にパートナーと交代しながら、書いた名詞を発音してください。

apple　rice　milk　egg　fruit　meat　cake　pizza　tomato
bread　book　money　coin　strawberry　paper　air　fish

Countable	Uncountable	Both
1._____	1._____	1._____
2._____	2._____	2._____
3._____	3._____	3._____
4._____	4._____	4._____
5._____	5._____	5._____
	6._____	
	7._____	

Exercise 2: Work with a partner. Take turns reading the sentences and questions below out loud. Write "**How many**" or "**How much**" on the lines to make the questions. Check your answers with your teacher. Then take turns asking and answering the questions. Make up your own answers. Write your partner's answers on the lines after the questions.　ペアで行います。1 ～ 10 の質問の下線部に How many か How much の適切な方を入れて、大きな声で読み上げましょう。先生と答え合わせをしてから、パートナーと質問しあいましょう。答えは自分たちで考えてください。パートナーの答えを各質問の下の下線部に文章で書き込んでください。

1. We need some coffee. _____ do we need?

   _____

2. We want some apples. _____ should we buy?

   _____

3. _____ bottles of beer are in the refrigerator?

   _____

4. _____ sugar do you like in your tea?

   _____

5. _____ fruit do you eat in a week?

   _____

6. _____ children do your parents have?

   _____

7. _____ sleep do you get each night?

   _____

8. _____ money do you have with you today?

   _____

9. _____ eggs do you usually buy at the store?

   _____

10. _____ loose-leaf paper do you usually bring to class?

    _____

III. Conversation 2

Read and listen to the conversation below. Then take turns practicing it with a partner, changing roles each time. 会話を聞き、パートナーと一緒に練習しましょう。1度読み終えたら役を交代してもう1度練習します。

Ayaka and John continue talking on the way home from the supermarket.
アヤカとジョンはスーパーからの帰り道で話をしています。

09

John: So, how many people are coming to your friend's birthday party?

Ayaka: I'm inviting about ten people.

John: That means a lot of food! Are you making all of it by yourself?

Ayaka: I think I can. I love cooking.

John: If you need some help, I can come early.

Ayaka: Thanks. If you can come an hour early, that would be great!

John: You can count on me*! I like to cook.

Ayaka: Really? What is your favorite thing to make?

John: Fried chicken! I add* a little soy sauce to the batter*.

Ayaka: Sounds great! Can you make some for the party?

John: Sure. Shall I bring some drinks, too?

Ayaka: I think we have enough, thanks.

John: OK! Then, see you tomorrow.

Ayaka: All right, see you! I'm looking forward to* your fried chicken!

* count on ～ ～に任せる　add 加える　batter（液状の）生地・衣　look forward to ～ ～を楽しみにして待つ

Practice: With a partner, write a conversation based on **Conversation 2**. Fill in the blanks below with information about yourselves. Take turns reading your conversation out loud, changing roles each time.
パートナーと協力し、上の Conversation 2 をもとに、自分たちに関するオリジナル会話文を作成しましょう。書き終えたら声に出して2度練習します。大きくはっきりとした声で読み上げること。2度目は役を交代して読み上げましょう。

A: So, how many people are coming to your _____?

B: I'm inviting about _____ people.

A: That means _____. Are you making _____ yourself?

B: _____. I _____.

A: If you need some help, _____.

B: Thanks. If _____, that would be great!

A: You can count on me! I _____.

B: Really? What is your favorite thing to make?

A: _____! I _____.

B: Sounds great! _____?

A: Sure. Shall I bring _____?

B: _____.

A: OK! Then, see you _____.

B: All right, see you! I'm looking forward to _____!

Ⅳ. Active Learning: How to count uncountable nouns

How can we count uncountable nouns?　それでは「数えられない名詞」を数えたいときはどうすればよいでしょうか。「数えられない名詞」は、容器の名前や単位を使って表現することができます。

We can count uncountable nouns by counting the sections or containers they come in.

> **Quantity (a, two …) + container* (bag(s), cup(s), glass(es) …) + of + Uncountable noun**
> 数量　　　　　　　　　＋ 容器など　　　　　　　　　　　　　＋ of ＋ 数えられない名詞

Example: 例で見てみましょう。

> **a piece of pie … two pieces of pie (also: a slice of pie … two slices of pie)**
> **a bag of popcorn … two bags of popcorn**

Exercise 1: With a partner, match the uncountable nouns below with the appropriate counting words. Hint: Think about what containers the things come in. **Some nouns have more than one answer.**　ペアで行います。1 〜 12 の計量表現に合う名詞を下の A 〜 L から選んで下線部に書き入れましょう。2 つ以上の計量表現が使える名詞もあります。それぞれのものがどのような容器に入っているかがヒントです。

1. a bowl of ＿＿＿＿＿
2. a cup of ＿＿＿＿＿
3. a slice of ＿＿＿＿＿
4. a glass of ＿＿＿＿＿
5. a roll of ＿＿＿＿＿
6. a can of ＿＿＿＿＿
7. a bottle of ＿＿＿＿＿
8. a box of ＿＿＿＿＿
9. a piece of ＿＿＿＿＿
10. a carton of ＿＿＿＿＿
11. a tube of ＿＿＿＿＿
12. a bag of ＿＿＿＿＿

A. toothpaste*　B. cake　C. tea　D. cereal　E. wine　F. candy　G. rice
H. toilet paper　I. milk　J. bread　K. tuna fish　L. orange juice

* container 容器　toothpaste 歯磨き粉

Exercise 2: With a partner, fill in the blanks in the conversations below. Then take turns practicing each conversation, changing roles each time.　以下の会話を完成させましょう。終わったらペアで会話を練習しましょう。1 度目を終えたら役を交代してもう 1 度練習しましょう。

1. A: Let's make some *okonomiyaki* for our party. We will have to buy two ＿＿＿＿＿ of *okonomiyaki* mix and ＿＿＿＿＿ eggs.

   B: We will need some drinks, too. Shall we get a big ＿＿＿＿＿ of cola?

2. A: What do you usually have for breakfast?

   B: I usually have a ＿＿＿＿＿ of bread, ＿＿＿＿＿ fruit, and a ＿＿＿＿＿ of coffee. I also have a ＿＿＿＿＿ of milk. I sometimes have a ＿＿＿＿＿ of cereal instead of* bread.

3. A: Are you going shopping? Could you bring back a ＿＿＿＿＿ of paper towels*? I have only one ＿＿＿＿＿ left.

   B: OK. Do you need a ＿＿＿＿＿ of tissues, too?

* instead of 〜の変わりに　paper towels キッチン・ペーパー

41

Unit 5

How many people are there in your family?

There is / There are / It is / They are

I. Conversation 1

As you listen to the conversation below, fill in the missing parts. Check your answers with a partner and with your teacher. Repeat each line after your teacher, and then take turns practicing the conversation with your partner, changing roles each time. 会話を聞き、下の会話文の下線部を埋めましょう。パートナーと答えを確認してください。そのあと、先生と答え合わせをし、先生に続いて文を復唱してください。最後にパートナーと会話を練習しましょう。1度読み終えたら次は役を交代してもう1度行いましょう。

Ayaka and John talk in the morning before class.
アヤカとジョンは朝の授業前に話をしています。

🎧10

Ayaka: Hello, John. How are you (1)_____ _____?

John: Hi, Ayaka. I'm fine. How about you?

Ayaka: I'm (2)_____ _____, but I'm a little hungry. (3)_____ _____ a box lunch* in my bag. My mother makes a box lunch for everyone in my family. I want to eat some of mine before class.

John: How nice! (4)_____ _____ people are there in your family, by the way*?

Ayaka: (5)_____ _____ seven people in my family. (6)_____ _____ my father, my mother, my older sister, my two younger brothers, my grandmother, and me.

John: Wow, you (7)_____ a big family!

Ayaka: How about you, John?

John: In my family, (8)_____ _____ only four people—my parents, my brother, and me.

Ayaka: Is your brother (9)_____ than you?

John: No, he's (10)_____. He's my little brother.

Ayaka: I see.

* box lunch お弁当　by the way ところで

Questions: Work with a partner. Take turns asking and answering the questions below about **Conversation 1**. Answer **in full sentences**. Write the answers on the lines using "There is," "There are," or "They are." ペアで行います。Conversation 1 の会話について、下の質問をし、答えを書き取りましょう。答えるときは、There is / There are あるいは It is / They are の内、適切なものを用いて、単語ではなく文章（主語・述語がはいった文）で答えること。1 人だけが聞いたり 1 人だけが答えたりするのではなく、交互に質問し、2 人とも全ての質問をし、全ての質問に答えるようにすること。

1. What's in Ayaka's bag?

   _____

2. How many people are there in Ayaka's family?

   _____

3. Who are the people in Ayaka's family?

   _____

4. How many people are in John's family?

   _____

5. Who are the people in John's family?

   _____

Practice: With a partner write a conversation based on **Conversation 1**. Fill in the blanks below with information about yourselves. Take turns reading your conversation out loud, changing roles each time. パートナーと協力して空欄を埋め、自分たちに関するオリジナル会話文を作りましょう。書き終えたら声に出して 2 度練習します。大きくはっきりとした声で読み上げること。2 度目は役を交代して読み上げましょう。

A: Hello, _____. How are you _____?

B: Hi, _____. I'm _____. How about you?

A: I'm _____, but I'm a little _____. There _____ in my bag.
   I want to _____.

B: _____. How many people are there in your family, by the way?

A: There are _____ people in my family. They are my _____
   _____, and me. _____.

B: Sounds like you have _____ family.

A: How about you? How many _____?

B: In my family, there are _____ people. They are my _____
   _____, and me.

A: Is your _____?

B: _____. _____.

A: I see.

* 兄弟姉妹がいない場合：ひとりっ子＝ an only child. または、"I dont have any brothers or sisters." と言います。
  「ひとりっ子ですか」と聞く場合は "Are you an only child?" です。

II. Grammar & Practice: There is … / There are …

"There is" and "There are" are used to describe things that exist. After writing or saying "There is," use a singular or uncountable noun. After "There are," use a plural noun. If the first subject in a list is singular, use "There is." If the first subject is plural, use " there are."　"There is" と "There are" は、何かがそこに「ある」「いる」ことを示すために使います。There is のあとには単数形が、There are の後には複数形がきます。いくつかの種類のものが「ある」ときには、There is / There are のすぐ後ろにくる名詞が単数形なら There is、複数形なら There are を使います。下の例を見てください。

> In my house, there is a living room, a dining room, a kitchen, and three bedrooms.
> In my house, there are three bedrooms, a kitchen, a living room, and a dining room.

Exercise 1: Work with a partner, fill in the blank in each sentence below with "There is" or "There are." Take turns saying each sentence after you complete it.　パートナーと一緒に "There is" か "There are" を下線部に書き入れましょう。書き終わったら声に出して読み上げましょう。

1. _____ a pencil case and some pencils in my bag.

2. _____ three candy bars in the drawer.

3. In my room, _____ a desk, some bookcases, and a bed.

4. _____ some apples on the table.

5. _____ some food in my bag.

Exercise 2: With a partner, read the grammar section on page 107 in the **Appendix** (Unit 5 There is/There are/It is/They are). Then work together to fill in the blanks in the sentences below with: **There is/There isn't/There are/There aren't/They are(n't)/It is(n't)**. Some sentences are questions, so the order of the verb and **There/It is** are reversed.: **Are there …? Is it …?** Take turns reading each sentence as you complete it.　ペアで行います。付録 107 ページの　『『いる』『ある』の表現と It is / They are との違い」をよく読んでから下記の 1 ～ 14 の空欄に、There is / There isn't / There are / There aren't / They are / They aren't / It is / It isn't のうち適切なものを書き入れましょう。中には質問もあります。質問の場合は、例えば There is は Is there となりますね。文章を完成させながら声にだして読み上げましょう。交代で読み上げてください。

1. _____ seven people in my family. _____ my parents, my grandmother, my two brothers, and me.

2. In our hospital, _____ 30 doctors now.

3. I like cheese crackers. _____ very good!

4. _____ a microwave* in your room?

5. _____ many patients* in the waiting room. Only a few are here.

6. What's that? _____ my bicycle.

7. _____ many students in your class?

8. _____ some coffee in the pot.

9. _____ cold today.

10. _____ a problem? I saw you arguing* with someone.

11. _____ any pictures in this classroom.

12. What's that? _____ the book we use for our English class this year.

13. _____ the students from Australia.

14. _____ a vending machine* on this floor. I looked for one, but I couldn't find* one.

* microwave 電子レンジ   patients 患者   argue 口げんかする・口論する   vending machine 自動販売機   find 見つける

III. Conversation 2

Read and listen to the conversation below. Then take turns practicing it with a partner two times, changing roles each time.   会話を聞き、パートナーと一緒に練習しましょう。1度読み終えたら役を交代してもう1度練習します。

Ayaka and John talk after class.   アヤカとジョンが授業の後に話をしています。   🎧11

Ayaka: Wow! You have a really big backpack, John!

John:　I have many classes, so I have a lot of books.

Ayaka: Is there a computer in your backpack, too?

John:　Yes. I use it to take notes* and write email to my family and friends. Do you have a computer with you?

Ayaka: No, it's at home. I can use my cell phone for communicating with my friends and family. I still like to write notes for my classes in my notebook.

John:　But what do you have in your bag? It looks heavy.

Ayaka: There are all of my books, of course, and all of my notebooks. There is also my pencil case, my box lunch, and a thermos. There are also some snacks.

John:　Oh! I just remembered something. There isn't any food in my bag, and there aren't any snacks, either! I'm hungry. I'll go to the convenience store. See you later, Ayaka.

* take notes メモを取る

Practice: With a partner write a conversation based on **Conversation 2**. Fill in the blanks below with information about yourselves. Take turns reading your conversation out loud, changing roles each time.
パートナーと協力し、上の Conversation 2 をもとに、自分たちに関するオリジナル会話文を作成しましょう。書き終えたら声に出して 2 度練習します。大きくはっきりとした声で読み上げること。2 度目は役を交代して読み上げましょう。

A:　Wow! You really have a big _____!

B:　I have many _____, so there are a lot of _____ I have to _____.

A:　Is there a _____ in your _____, too?

B:　Yes. I have to _____ and _____. Do you have _____ with you?

A:　_____. I use _____ for _____.

B:　What is there in your _____? It looks _____.

A:　There are _____. There is also _____.

B:　Oh no! There isn't/aren't any _____ in my _____. I'll _____ now. See you later.

IV. Active Learning: **There is / There are / It is / They are**

Exercise 1: Ask a partner the questions below. Write your partner's answers on the lines. Use "**There is**," "**There are**" to start your first sentence. Add more information to describe each item, starting with "**It is**," or "**They are**." Say five things for each question. Then change roles. Write your partner's answers on the lines. パートナーに下記の 3 つの質問をします。答えは There is / There are で始めます。それぞれの質問に対し、5 つのものを考え、声にだして主語と述語動詞を含む文章で答えましょう。その後、相手の答えを文章で下線部に書き入れてください。

What's in the classroom?

Example: There is a blackboard in the classroom. It's in the front of the room.

1. _____ _____
2. _____ _____
3. _____ _____
4. _____ _____
5. _____ _____

What's in your bag?

Example: There are candies in her bag. They are lemon-flavored.

1. _____ _____
2. _____ _____
3. _____ _____
4. _____ _____
5. _____ _____

What's in your room at home?

Example: There is a computer in his room. It is an Apple computer.

1. _____ _____
2. _____ _____
3. _____ _____
4. _____ _____
5. _____ _____

Exercise 2: Work together with another pair. Tell the others about the items in your partner's bag and in his/her room at home. As you listen to the others, write their answers on the lines, as in the **Example**.

もう1組のペアと一緒に行います。例にしたがって、あなたのパートナーのバッグの中にあるものを、もう1組のペア2人に話します。相手のペアの2人が話したものについては文章で下線部に書き込んでください。

Example: "In Kaito's bag, there is a blue pencil case, ..."

Member #1: _____

_____

_____

_____

_____

Member #2: _____

_____

_____

_____

_____

When is your report due?

Cardinal & Ordinal Numbers

I. Conversation 1

As you listen to the conversation below, fill in the missing parts. Check your answers with a partner and with your teacher. Repeat each line after your teacher, and then take turns practicing the conversation with your partner, changing roles each time.　会話を聞き、下の会話文の下線部を埋めましょう。パートナーと答えを確認してください。そのあと、先生と答え合わせをし、先生に続いて文を復唱してください。最後にパートナーと会話を練習しましょう。1度読み終えたら次は役を交代してもう1度行いましょう。

Ayaka and John are talking in the cafeteria.　アヤカとジョンがカフェで話をしています。　🎧12

Ayaka: Hi, John. What are you (1)_____?

John: I'm studying for my midterm* test for History class. It's on (2)_____
_____. What are you doing?

Ayaka: I'm (3)_____ my lunch. Are you (4)_____ lunch soon?

John: Yeah, I think so.

Ayaka: What are you (5)_____?

John: Maybe I'll have today's set lunch*. It's cheap, only (6)_____ yen. How about you?

Ayaka: I'm thinking of having chicken and egg on rice* with *miso* soup.

John: The lunch (7)_____ with salad and a drink. Pretty good!

Ayaka: The chicken and egg on rice is (8)_____ yen.

John: That sounds good.

Ayaka: Yeah, but actually, I'm on a diet. So I think I'll get chicken salad. That's only

(9)_____ yen. It has fewer* calories and costs less*.

John: That (10)_____ better.

　　* midterm 学期の中間　today's set lunch 日替りランチ　chicken and egg on rice 親子丼　fewer/less より少ない

Questions: Work with a partner. Take turns asking and answering the questions below about **Conversation 1**. Answer **in full sentences**, and write the answers on the lines.　ペアで行います。Conversation 1の会話について、下の質問をし、答えを書き取りましょう。答えるときは、単語ではなく文章（主語・述語動詞が入った文）で答えること。1人だけが聞いたり1人だけが答えたりするのではなく、交互に質問し、2人とも全ての質問をし、全ての質問に答えるようにすること。

1. What is John doing?

   _____

2. What is Ayaka doing?

   _____

3. What is John having for lunch? How much is it?

   _____

4. What is Ayaka thinking of having for lunch?

   _____

5. What did she finally decide to get? Why?

   _____

   _____

Practice: With a partner, write a conversation based on **Conversation 1**. Fill in the blanks below with information about yourselves. Take turns reading your conversation out loud, changing roles each time. パートナーと協力して空欄を埋め、自分たちに関するオリジナル会話文を作りましょう。書き終えたら声に出して2度練習します。大きくはっきりとした声で読み上げること。2度目は役を交代して読み上げましょう。

A: Hi, _____. What are you doing?

B: I'm _____. It's _____. What are you doing?

A: I'm _____. Are you _____?

B: _____.

A: What are you _____?

B: _____. _____ yen. How about you?

A: _____.

B: _____.

A: It costs/They cost _____.

B: _____.

II. Grammar & Practice: Cardinal Numbers 基数

Read the **Appendix** on pages 109-110 (Unit 6 Cardinal & Ordinal Numbers) and look at the numbers below. Repeat them after your teacher. 付録 109-110 ページの「数」を読み、下の数（基数）と英語での読み方を見てください。先生の後について読み上げてください。

---

1. **25.5** (twenty-five point five)
2. **100** (one hundred/a hundred)
3. **1,000** (one thousand/a thousand)
4. **10,000** (ten thousand)
5. **100,000** (one/a hundred thousand)
6. **1,000,000** (one million/a million)
7. **10,000,000** (ten million)
8. **100,000,000** (one/a hundred million)
9. **1,000,000,000** (one billion/a billion)
10. **103** (one hundred [and] three) (Or: Room one oh three)
11. **9,821** (nine thousand, eight hundred [and] twenty-one)
12. **8,661,312** (eight million, six hundred sixty-one thousand, three hundred [and] twelve)
13. **2,348,511,020** (two billion, three hundred forty-eight million, five hundred eleven thousand and twenty)

Exercise 1: Your teacher will read five numbers to you. Write the numbers on the lines below. (You don't have to spell out the numbers.) 先生が5つの数を読み上げます。聞き取って下線部に書き入れましょう（数字で書いてください）。

1. _____   2. _____

3. _____   4. _____

5. _____

Exercise 2: Work with a partner. Each of you think of five numbers and write them on the lines on the left. Then take turns reading your numbers out loud to each other. As your partner reads his/her numbers, write them on the lines on the right. ペアで行います。それぞれ、数を5つずつ考えて左側の下線部に書いてください。その後、パートナーに対して交代で数を英語で読み上げます。相手の数を聞き取って、右側の下線部に書き出してください。

Your numbers:	Your partner's numbers:
1. _____	_____
2. _____	_____
3. _____	_____
4. _____	_____
5. _____	_____

Exercise 3: Work with a partner. Ask and answer the questions below. Write your partner's answers on the lines. **This time, spell out the numbers.** ペアで行います。パートナーに 1 〜 7 の A の質問をしてください。相手の答えを下線部に書き入れてください。**今回は、数は数字ではなく文字におこして書きましょう（例：6 → six）。**

1. A: How tall are you?

   B: I'm _____ tall.

2. A: What's your shoe size?

   B: It's _____ .

3. A: How far do you live from this school?

   B: I live about _____ from this school.

4. A: How many people are in this room now?

   B: There are _____ people in this room now.

5. A: How many people are there living in Tokyo?

   B: _____

   _____ .

6. A: How many people are there in Japan? (the population)

   B: _____

   _____ .

7. A: How many people are there in the world?

   B: _____

   _____ .

III. Conversation 2

Listen to the conversation below. Then take turns practicing it with a partner, changing roles each time.
会話を聞き、パートナーと一緒に練習しましょう。1度読み終えたら役を交代してもう1度練習します。

Ayaka and John talk after class again.　アヤカとジョンは授業の後に再び話をしています。　13

Ayaka: What's the date today?

John:　It's May 21st. Why do you ask?

Ayaka: My report is due* on May 25th. I have only a couple of days to finish.

John:　What is your report on?

Ayaka: It's on the recent election in Japan.

John:　It sounds very complicated*.

Ayaka: It is! The report has to be 1,000 characters long.

John:　That sounds* long. Is that about 500 English words?

Ayaka: Maybe. It's about four pages in Japanese.

John:　That doesn't sound too long, but I know how difficult Japanese is.

* due 期限である　complicated 複雑な　sound(s) 〜のように思われる

Practice: With a partner, write a conversation based on **Conversation 2**. Fill in the blanks below with information about yourselves. Take turns reading your conversation out loud, changing roles each time.
パートナーと協力して、上の Conversation 2 をもとに、自分たちに関するオリジナル会話文を作成しましょう。書き終えたら声に出して2度練習します。大きくはっきりとした声で読み上げること。2度目は役を交代して読み上げましょう。

A:　What's the date _____?

B:　It's _____. Why do you ask?

A:　My _____ is due on _____. I _____.

B:　What is your _____ on?

A:　It's on _____.

B:　That sounds _____.

A:　It is! The _____ has to be _____.

B:　That sounds _____. Is that about _____?

A:　I think it will be about _____.

B:　That sounds _____. I know _____.

52

IV. Active Learning: **Ordinal Numbers** 序数

Read the **Appendix** on page 110 and repeat the dates in the box below after your teacher. 付録 110 ページの「序数」の部分を読み、先生の後について、下記の日付を読み上げましょう。

Month:	Date:	
January	1st	first
February	2nd	second
March	3rd	third
April	4th	fourth
May	5th	fifth
June	8th	eighth
July	9th	ninth
August	12th	twelfth
September	20th	twentieth
October	21st	twenty-first
November	22nd	twenty-second
December	23rd	twenty-third
	25th	twenty-fifth
	30th	thirtieth

Exercise 1: With a partner, take turns asking and answering the questions below. Spell out the months and dates. For 11 and 12, make up your own questions to ask your partner. Write your partner's answers on the lines. ペアで行います。それぞれの相手に 1 ～ 10 の質問をします。相手の言った答えを下線部に書き込みましょう。月と日付は数字ではなく、文字におこして書きましょう。11 と 12 の質問は自分たちでそれぞれ考え、相手の答えを下線部に書きましょう。

1. What's the sixth month? It's _____.

2. What's the fourth month? _____.

3. What's the eighth month? _____.

4. When is Valentine's Day? It's on _____.

5. When's Girls' Day? _____.

6. When's Children's Day? (Boys' Day) _____.

7. When's Halloween? _____.

8. When's Christmas Day? _____.

9. When's Culture Day? (文化の日) _____.

10. When's your next test? _____.

11. (own question:) _____?

    (answer:) _____.

12. (own question:) _____?

    (answer:) _____.

Exercise 2: Ask your partner the following questions. Write his/her answers on the lines. Spell out the numbers.　ペアで行います。パートナーに 1 ～ 5 の A の質問をしてください。聞き取った答えを B の空欄に書き込みましょう。数は数字ではなく、文字におこしてください。

1. A: When did you graduate from high school?

   B: I graduated from high school _____

   _____ .

2. A: When is your birthday?

   B: _____ .

3. A: What's the date next Monday?

   B: _____ .

4. A: When did this semester* start?

   B: It started on _____ .

5. A: When is your next test (in any class)?

   B: _____ .

   * semester 学期

Go over the dates with your teacher.　先生と答えを確認しましょう。

54

● **Review Game**

Work with a group, but use only one book. Follow these instructions:
下記の 1 ～ 4 の指示に従い、グループで行います。教科書は 1 冊だけ使って構いません。（コインが必要です）

1. Use a small object such as an eraser or a piece of paper as a marker.
    消しゴムや付箋のような小さなものを 1 つ用意してください。駒として使います。

2. Play "rock, paper, scissors" to decide who goes first. Take turns moving your marker.
    ジャンケンをして順番を決めます。表の 1 から順に交代で進めます。

3. Each player takes a turn by flipping a coin. If the coin lands face up, move two spaces. If the coin lands tails up, move one space.
    各プレイヤーが交代でコインを投げます。コインが表の場合は 2 つ進めてください。コインが裏の場合は 1 つしか進めません。

4. When you land on a space, ask and answer the question on it. Answer **in a full sentence**.
    とまったマスの質問を読み上げて、正しい英文で答えましょう。

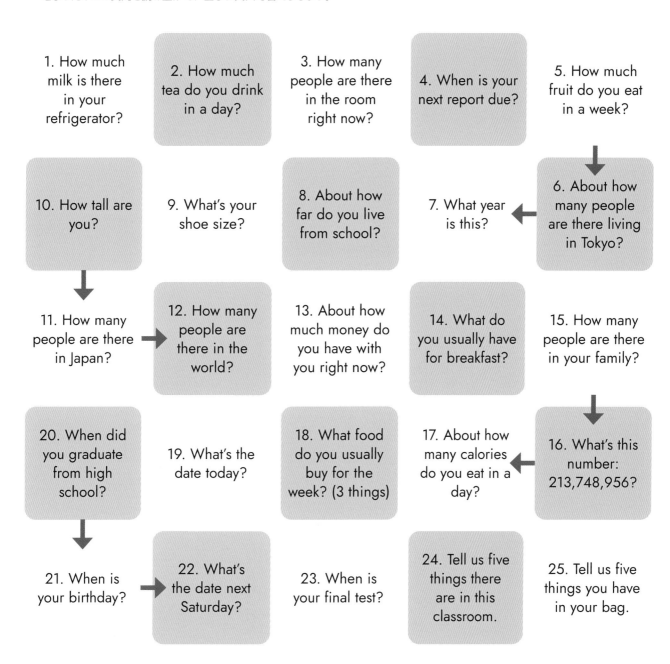

1. How much milk is there in your refrigerator?

2. How much tea do you drink in a day?

3. How many people are there in the room right now?

4. When is your next report due?

5. How much fruit do you eat in a week?

6. About how many people are there living in Tokyo?

7. What year is this?

8. About how far do you live from school?

9. What's your shoe size?

10. How tall are you?

11. How many people are there in Japan?

12. How many people are there in the world?

13. About how much money do you have with you right now?

14. What do you usually have for breakfast?

15. How many people are there in your family?

16. What's this number: 213,748,956?

17. About how many calories do you eat in a day?

18. What food do you usually buy for the week? (3 things)

19. What's the date today?

20. When did you graduate from high school?

21. When is your birthday?

22. What's the date next Saturday?

23. When is your final test?

24. Tell us five things there are in this classroom.

25. Tell us five things you have in your bag.

Part A: Work with a partner. On the lines below, write how to count the uncountable nouns, as in the example. Then take turns saying your answers out loud. ペアで行います。例に従って、数えられない名詞を数えられる言い方にしましょう。その後それぞれの答えを読み上げてください。

Example: <u>a slice of</u> cheese

1. _____ apple juice
2. _____ bread
3. _____ popcorn
4. _____ coffee
5. _____ cake

6. _____ rice
7. _____ toilet paper
8. _____ tuna fish
9. _____ water
10. _____ ointment*

* ointment 軟膏

Part B: Work with a partner. Make sentences by filling in the blanks with the most appropriate of these phrases: **There is/There isn't/There are/There aren't/They are(n't)/or It is(n't).** Some of these are in question form. ペアで行います。下記の 1 〜 14 の空欄に、There is / There isn't / There are / There aren't / They are / They aren't / It is / It isn't のうち適切なものを書き入れましょう。中には質問もあるので気を付けましょう。

1. _____ hot today.

2. _____ a restroom on this floor. I looked for one, but I couldn't find one.

3. _____ many students in your class?

4. _____ a nice car. I don't like it.

5. _____ many people in the gym.

6. Who are those students? _____ the students from New Zealand.

7. _____ a computer in this room?

8. _____ any TVs in their house.

9. _____ four people in my family. _____ my parents, my brother, and me.

10. _____ any trouble? I saw you arguing*with someone.

11. _____ some coffee in the pot.

12. What's that? _____ my new bicycle.

13. I like potato chips. _____ very tasty!

14. In our school, _____ 30 teachers.

* argue 言い合う

Part C: With your partner, take turns asking and answering the questions below. Write the answers **in full sentences**. Spell out the dates.　ペアで行います。交代で相手に 1 ～ 12 の質問をします。相手の言った答えを下線部に書き込みましょう。主語と述語動詞を含む**文章にして書き込むこと**。**日付は数字ではなく、文字におこして書きましょう。**

1. What's the third month of the year?
   It's _____ .

2. What's the sixth month of the year?
   _____ .

3. What's the ninth month of the year?
   _____ .

4. When is Valentine's Day?
   It's on _____ .

5. When's Children's Day?
   _____ .

6. When's Sports Day this year?（スポーツの日）
   _____ .

7. When's Christmas Eve?
   _____ .

8. When's Labor Thanksgiving Day?（勤労感謝の日）
   _____ .

9. When's New Year's Day?
   _____ .

10. When does the school year begin?
    _____ .

11. When is Marine Day this year?（海の日）
    _____ .

12. When is your birthday?
    _____ .

How was your weekend?

Past Tense

I. Conversation 1

As you listen to the conversation below, fill in the missing parts. Check your answers with a partner and with your teacher. Repeat each line after your teacher, and then take turns practicing the conversation with your partner, changing roles each time. 会話を聞き、下の会話文の下線部を埋めましょう。パートナーと答えを確認してください。そのあと、先生と答え合わせをし、先生に続いて文を復唱してください。最後にパートナーと会話を練習しましょう。1度読み終えたら次は役を交代してもう1度行いましょう。

Ayaka and John talk about last weekend. アヤカとジョンは先週末のことを話しています。　🎧14

Ayaka: Hello, John. Nice to see you. How (1)_____ your weekend?

John: Oh, hi, Ayaka. My weekend was great!

Ayaka: What (2)_____ you do?

John: My brother was on a business trip* to Japan last week, and he (3)_____ with me this weekend. So we visited Asakusa and (4)_____ around the Skytree area.

Ayaka: How nice! Did you (5)_____ a fortune slip* from the temple* at Asakusa?

John: We sure did! I (6)_____ the best luck. My brother's luck was only so-so. What did you do this weekend?

Ayaka: I just cleaned my room and (7)_____.

John: What did you study?

Ayaka: I studied Political Science* and English. (8)_____ both hard.

John: Yeah, I know. I had to do a lot of studying last week, because my brother

(9)_____ _____.

Ayaka: When did he leave?

John: He (10)_____ this morning.

* business trip 出張   fortune slip おみくじ   temple 寺   Political Science 政治学

Questions: Work with a partner. Take turns asking and answering the questions below about **Conversation 1**. Answer **in full sentences** and write the answers on the lines.   ペアで行います。Conversation 1 の会話について、下の質問をし、答えを書き取りましょう。答えるときは、単語ではなく文章（主語・述語がはいった文）で答えること。1 人だけが聞いたり 1 人だけが答えたりするのではなく、交互に質問し、2 人とも全ての質問をし、全ての質問に答えるようにすること。

1. How was John's weekend?

_____

2. Where did he and his brother go?

_____

3. What kind of luck did John and his brother get?

_____

4. What did Ayaka do this weekend?

_____

5. When did John's brother leave?

_____

Practice: With a partner, write a conversation based on **Conversation 1**. Fill in the blanks below with information about yourselves. Take turns reading your conversation out loud, changing roles each time.   パートナーと協力して空欄を埋め、自分たちに関するオリジナル会話文を作りましょう。書き終えたら声に出して 2 度練習します。大きくはっきりとした声で読み上げること。2 度目は役を交代して読み上げましょう。

A: Hello, _____. Nice to see you. How was your weekend?

B: Oh, hi, _____. My weekend was _____.

A: What did you do?

B: I _____.

A: _____! Did you _____?

B: _____. _____. What did you do last weekend*?

A: I _____.

B: What _____?

A: I _____.

* last weekend 先週末

II. Grammar & Practice: **Past tense** 過去形

Read the section in the **Appendix** (Unit 7, Past Tense) on page 111. Then go over the rules for past tense below with your teacher. 付録 111 ページの「過去形」をよく読み、先生と一緒に下の表で過去形の成り立ちについてみていきましょう。

Past-tense verb forms usually follow one of these patterns, depending on the type of verb.

Regular past-tense verb forms*:

　walk-**walked**, move-**moved**, start-**started**, stay-**stayed**, study-**studied**

Pronunciation* of regular past-tense verbs:

1. If verbs **end in voiceless*** sounds (**p, f, k, s, sh, ch, th**), the past is pronounced with a "**t**" sound ("**walked**").
2. If verbs **end in voiced*** sounds (**b, v, g, z, j, th, l, m, n, r, or e**), the past is pronounced with a "**d**" sound ("**moved**").
3. If verbs **end** in "**t**" or "**d**", the past sound is "**id**" ("**started**," "**ended**").

Irregular past-tense verb forms*:

1. sing-**sang** (i-a)
2. blow-**blew** ("**ew**" ending)
3. take-**took** ("**ook**" ending)
4. make-**made** (past tense ends with a "**d**" sound)
5. buy-**bought** ("**aught/ought**" ending)
6. sleep-**slept** ("**t**" ending)
7. cut-**cut** (**no change**)
8. Other verbs change in specific ways and must be memorized*: **be, see, go, do, come, run**, etc.

* regular verbs 規則動詞　pronunciation 発音　voiceless 無声音　voiced 有声音
irregular verbs 不規則動詞　memorize 暗記する

Exercise 1: With a partner, take turns saying the present and past tense forms of the irregular verbs in the box below. Write the past tense of the verbs. Continue on the next page. ペアで行います。1 〜 25 の動詞について、1 人がまず現在形を読み上げ、もう 1 人がその過去形を言います。その後、先ほど過去形を言った人が次の単語の現在形、というように順番に行っていきましょう。その後過去形を全て書き入れてください。

Example: (be) am, is, are ➡ was, were

Present	Past	Present	Past
1. break		**2.** bring	
3. catch		**4.** come	
5. choose		**6.** drink	
7. eat		**8.** find	
9. fly		**10.** get	
11. give		**12.** go	

13. have		**14.** hear	
15. keep		**16.** know	
17. lose		**18.** meet	
19. put		**20.** read	
21. say		**22.** see	
23. swim		**24.** think	
25. write			

Exercise 2: Work with a partner. Take turns reading the sentences below. Fill in the blanks with the past-tense forms of the words in parentheses.　ペアで行います。1〜20の（　　）内の動詞を正しい過去形に変えて順番に文章を読み上げてください。その後下線部に過去形の動詞を記入しましょう。

1.　It _____(rain) yesterday.

2.　We _____(live) in Tokyo when we _____(be) young.

3.　John _____(swim) in the ocean in the summer.

4.　They _____(see) her at the supermarket.

5.　Ayaka _____(drink) orange juice for breakfast.

6.　Mari _____(write) in her diary last night.

7.　Tom _____(read) a good book on the weekend.

8.　I _____(finish) my homework at 9:00 p.m.

9.　Mr. and Mrs. Smith _____(count) their money and _____(find) that they didn't have enough money to go to a restaurant.

10.　I _____(put) my wallet on the table, but somebody _____(take) it.

11.　Karen _____(use) her cell phone to call an ambulance*.

12.　We _____(fly) to Hokkaido last summer.

13.　Susan _____(keep) her diary in her bedroom drawer*.

14.　I don't know what she _____(say) to him to make him angry.

15.　Yuriko _____(know) why he was angry.

16.　My mother _____(fry) eggs for breakfast.

17.　The teacher _____(announce) that there will be a quiz next week.

18.　My brother _____(catch) a cold last week.

19.　Christine _____(play) the piano when she was in elementary school.

20.　Maria _____(want) to see a movie today, but she _____(have) a dentist appointment.

* ambulance 救急車　drawer 引き出し

III. Conversation 2

Listen to the conversation below. Then take turns practicing it with a partner, changing roles each time.
会話を聞き、パートナーと一緒に練習しましょう。1度読み終えたら役を交代してもう1度練習します。

Ayaka and John talk after the day's classes are finished.
アヤカとジョンは、1日の授業が終わったあとに話をしています。

15

John: How many classes did you have today, Ayaka?

Ayaka: I had two classes, European History and English Conversation. And you?

John: I had French, Biology, and Physics*.

Ayaka: How were they?

John: OK, I guess. Physics was tough. How were your classes?

Ayaka: European History was interesting, and, of course, I love English.

John: What did you do in your classes?

Ayaka: I reviewed some irregular* past-tense verb forms.

John: Which verbs did you review?

Ayaka: I forget most of them, but I remember some: brought, bought, and chose.

John: Those are important verbs to remember!

Ayaka: There are so many irregular past-tense verb forms to learn.

John: Actually, there aren't so many—only about 200 that we use every day. If you learn the most common* ones, you'll be a good English speaker.

Ayaka: Thanks for the advice*, John. I'll try to learn as many as I can.

* physics 物理学   irregular 不規則の   common 共通の   advice アドバイス、助言

Practice: With a partner, write a conversation based on **Conversation 2**. Fill in the blanks below with information about yourselves. Take turns reading your conversation out loud, changing roles each time.
パートナーと協力し、上の Conversation 2 をもとに、自分たちに関するオリジナル会話文を作成しましょう。書き終えたら声に出して2度練習します。大きくはっきりとした声で読み上げること。2度目は役を交代して読み上げましょう。

A: How many classes did you have _____?

B: I had _____. And you?

A: I had _____.

B: How was/were your class(es)?

A: _____. _____ for me. And your class(es)?

B: _____. _____.

A: What did you do in your classes?

B: _____. And you?

A: I _____.

IV. Active Learning

With a partner, take turns asking and answering the questions below. Write down your partner's answers **in full sentences**. Write in the third person using: He/She/His/Her ...　ペアで行います。パートナーに 1 〜 8 の質問をしましょう。質問ごとに交互に聞き合います。相手の答えは完全な文章で書き込みましょう。相手に尋ねる時は二人称（You/Your）ですが、書く時は三人称（He/She/His/Her）を使ってください。

1. What things did you bring with you to class today?

   _____

2. What did you buy last weekend?

   _____

3. What did you give your best friend for his/her birthday?

   _____

4. Who(m) did you meet last week?

   _____

5. How long did you sleep last night?

   _____

6. What time did you come to school today?

   _____

7. How long did you study last night?

   _____

8. How long did you work on your last report?

   _____

Ask your partner two more questions of your own using past-tense verb forms.

質問 9 と 10 は過去形を使って質問から考えてください。

9. _____?

   _____

10. _____?

    _____

What time is your first class?

Time

I. Conversation 1

As you listen to the conversation below, fill in the missing parts. Check your answers with a partner. Then check your answers with your teacher. Repeat each line after your teacher, and then take turns practicing the conversation with your partner, changing roles each time.　会話を聞き、下の会話文の下線部を埋めましょう。パートナーと答えを確認してください。そのあと、先生と答え合わせをし、先生に続いて文を復唱してください。最後にパートナーと会話を練習しましょう。1度読み終えたら次は役を交代してもう1度行いましょう。

Ayaka and John talk about their school schedules.
アヤカとジョンが大学での時間割について話をしています。

16

John:　What class did you have first period* today, Ayaka?

Ayaka:　I had Intermediate English (1)_____, with Professor Takeo. How about you?

John:　I had Japanese in the Foreign (2)_____ Department*.

Ayaka:　How was your class?

John:　It was good, but my instructor gives (3)_____ _____ _____

homework. How many classes do you have this semester*?

Ayaka:　I have (4)_____ classes altogether. And you?

John:　I have 14 classes, for (5)_____ credits*. How many classes do you have today?

Ayaka:　Let's see … I have first and second periods and then there's lunch at ten after

(6)_____.

John: Oh, I thought lunch (7)_____ at noon*.

Ayaka: Each class is (8)_____ minutes long, remember?

John: Oh, yeah, that's right. After lunch, I have (9)_____ period and fourth period, for a total of six hours of classes today!

Ayaka: Wow! You have a long day! And lunch is only (10)_____ minutes long.

John: I know!

* period 時限　department 学部　semester 学期　credit 単位　noon 正午

Questions: Work with a partner. Take turns asking and answering the questions about **Conversation 1**. Answer **in full sentences** and write the answers on the lines. ペアで行います。Conversation 1 の会話について、下の質問をし、答えを書き取りましょう。答えるときは、単語ではなく文章（主語・述語がはいった文）で答えること。1 人だけが聞いたり 1 人だけが答えたりするのではなく、交互に質問し、2 人とも全ての質問をし、全ての質問に答えるようにすること。

1. What class did Ayaka have first period? _____

2. How many classes does John have in total*? _____

3. When is lunch at their school? _____

4. How many classes does John have today? _____

5. How long is lunch at their school? _____

* in total 全部で

Practice: With a partner, write a conversation based on **Conversation 1**. Fill in the blanks below with information about yourselves. Take turns reading your conversation out loud, changing roles each time. パートナーと協力して空欄を埋め、自分たちに関するオリジナル会話文を作りましょう。書き終えたら声に出して 2 度練習します。大きくはっきりとした声で読み上げること。2 度目は役を交代して読み上げましょう。

A: What classes did/do you have today?

B: I had/have _____. And you?

A: I had/have _____. What periods do/did you have today?

B: I have/had _____ (and) _____ period(s). And you?

A: I have/had _____, _____ (and) _____ period(s). How many classes do you have this semester?

B: I have _____ classes. How about you?

A: I have _____ classes for _____ credits.

B: I have _____ credits.

II. Grammar & Practice: **Telling time**

There are two ways to tell the time in English. One way is to say the hours first. The second way is to say the minutes first, which is the most natural way in daily conversation. Read the **Appendix** on page 113 (Unit 8 Time) and look at the two ways to tell the time below. Practice saying both ways with your teacher. 英語には 2 通りの時刻の伝え方があります。1 つ目は「〜時」を先に言うもので、2 つ目は「〜分」を先に言うものです。この 2 つ目の「〜分」が先の言い方は日常生活で最もよく使われます。付録 113 ページの「時間の表現」をよく読み、また下の表で、2 種類の伝え方を確認しましょう。どちらの種類の表現も先生と一緒に練習しましょう。

Hours first (formal)	Minutes first (conversational)
1:05 = one oh five	five after one/five past one
1:10 = one ten	ten after one/ten past one
1:15 = one fifteen	a quarter after one/a quarter past one
1:30 = one thirty	half past one
1:35 = one thirty-five	twenty-five to two
1:45 = one forty-five	a quarter to two

- When somebody asks you the time—for example, "What's the time?" or "What time is it now?"—you should answer: 誰かに時間を聞かれたら下のように答えましょう。聞き方にも 2 つあります。

  "**It's** ten after/past four." OR "**It's** a quarter to five."

- When somebody asks you the time that something **happens**—for example, "What time do you have dinner?" or "What time does the first class start?"—you should answer with **at**. 何かを何時に行うか、何が何時に起こるか、についての質問には、at を使って答えます。

  Examples:
  "I have dinner **at** half past seven." OR "My first class starts **at** nine o'clock."

- In English, only the military and some official agencies use the 24-hour clock. We don't normally use it in everyday conversation. So we say: "It's one/1:00 p.m." and not 13:00 or "thirteen-hundred hours." 24 時間制に従って時刻を表現するのは、米国の官庁の一部や軍などにおいてだけです。一般的な会話においては、普通は 12 時間制の表現が a.m./p.m. と共に使われます。

Exercise 1: Draw hands on the clocks below to show four different times. Ask your partner, "**What time is it?**" for each clock. Answer in the natural conversational way. Spell out the times on the lines below.
まずは下の時計に好きな時刻を書き込みましょう。その後パートナーに何時かを英語で答えてもらいます。前ページの表の右側の会話調（conversational）の時刻表現を使いましょう。最後に 1 〜 4 の下線部にそれらの時刻を英語で書き込んでください。

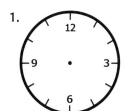 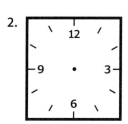 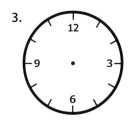 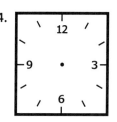

1. It's _____ .

2. It's _____ .

3. It's _____ .

4. It's _____ .

Exercise 2: Now ask your partner about the beginning, ending, opening, and closing times below. Spell out the times.　1 〜 2 の時計の絵を参考に、開始時間と終了時間についてパートナーに質問しましょう。パートナーの答えを下線部に書いてください。時刻は数字をつかわずに文字におこしてください。

1.

  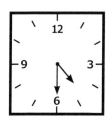

You:　　What time does the bank open?

Partner: _____ .

You:　　What time does it close?

Partner: _____ .

2.

  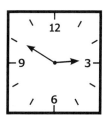

You:　　What time does the movie begin?

Partner: _____ .

You:　　What time does it end?

Partner: _____ .

III. Conversation 2

Listen to the conversation below. Then take turns practicing it with a partner two times, changing roles each time.　会話を聞き、パートナーと一緒に練習しましょう。1度読み終えたら役を交代してもう1度練習します。

Ayaka and John continue their conversation.　アヤカとジョンが会話を続けています。 17

> John:　What time does your next class start?
>
> Ayaka:　It starts at twenty to eleven. There are only ten minutes between classes.
>
> John:　I guess we'd better hurry.
>
> Ayaka:　What time do you finish classes today?
>
> John:　I finish at ten to six. I won't get home until about 7:30 tonight. What about you?
>
> Ayaka:　I get home at a quarter to eleven, because I have a part-time job.
>
> John:　Oh, where do you work?
>
> Ayaka:　I work at a convenience store near my house.
>
> John:　That sounds convenient. Is it hard work?
>
> Ayaka:　It's OK. I work about four hours a day, three days a week.
>
> John:　It's a good way to get a little pocket money*.

* pocket money お小遣い

Practice: With a partner, write a conversation based on **Conversation 2**. Fill in the blanks below with information about yourselves. Take turns reading your conversation out loud, changing roles each time. パートナーと協力し、上の Conversation 2 をもとに、自分たちに関するオリジナル会話文を作成しましょう。書き終えたら声に出して2度練習します。大きくはっきりとした声で読み上げること。2度目は役を交代して読み上げましょう。

A:　What time does your next class start?

B:　It starts _____ and finishes _____. What time do you finish classes today?

A:　I finish _____. When do you finish classes?

B:　I finish _____. When do you get home today?

A:　I get home _____. And you?

B:　I get home _____. What do you usually do after school?

A:　I usually _____. And you?

B:　I _____.

A:　That sounds _____.

IV. Active Learning

Exercise 1: With a partner, take turns asking and answering the questions below about your daily schedules. Write your partner's answers **in full sentences**, using, for example, "He/She got up at …" Use the natural conversation way to tell time and spell out the times as you write them. For numbers 11 and 12 below, make up two questions of your own to ask your partner.　ペアで行います。1日のスケジュールについてパートナーに1〜10の質問をしましょう。パートナーの答えを単語ではなく文章で答えてください（例：He/She got up at…）。会話調での時刻表現を使い、パートナーの答えは、数字ではなく文字におこして下線部に書き込みましょう。11と12は質問も考えてください。

1. What time did you get up this morning? _____.

2. What time did you eat breakfast? _____.

3. What time did you leave for school? _____.

4. What time did you arrive at school? _____.

5. What time do you usually have lunch? _____.

6. What time do you leave school today? _____.

7. What time do you get home today? _____.

8. What time do you usually have dinner? _____.

9. What time do you usually take a bath or shower?

    _____.

10. What time do you usually go to bed? _____.

11. _____? _____.

12. _____? _____.

Exercise 2: Now tell another pair about your partner's schedule. As the other members tell you about their partners' schedules, write notes in the spaces provided below. Write the other pair's members' names in the parentheses.　次はもう1組のペアと一緒に4人で行います。他のペアの2人に、自分のパートナーのスケジュールを話してください。他のペアの1人がそのパートナーのスケジュールについて話している時は、下線部に書き出しましょう。（　　）内には、他のペアの2人の名前をそれぞれ記入してください。

Example: (Hiro) got up at 6:30, ate breakfast at …

Other member 1: (　　　　　　) _____

_____

_____

_____

Other member 2: (　　　　　　) _____

_____

_____

_____

Have you ever been to Kyoto?

Present Perfect

Paris

Versailles

I. Conversation 1

As you listen to the conversation below, fill in the missing parts. Check your answers with a partner and with your teacher. Repeat each line after your teacher, and then take turns practicing the conversation with your partner, changing roles each time.　会話を聞き、下の会話文の下線部を埋めましょう。パートナーと答えを確認してください。そのあと、先生と答え合わせをし、先生に続いて文を復唱してください。最後にパートナーと会話を練習しましょう。1度読み終えたら次は役を交代してもう1度行いましょう。

Ayaka talks to John after her history class.　歴史学の授業の後、アヤカがジョンに話かけています。　🎧18

Ayaka: John, have you ever (1)_____ to Europe?

John:　Yes, I've been to France (2)_____ _____. One of my cousins lives there.

Ayaka: That's lucky! I would love to visit Paris. I've (3)_____ been there.

John:　There are a lot of (4)_____ to see in Paris. What would you like to do most there?

Ayaka: I'd like to visit Versailles*. My teacher was (5)_____ about its history today. It sounds very interesting. She has (6)_____ Europe lots of times.

John:　I've been to Versailles (7)_____. I went there in 2015. It was one of the best places I've ever (8)_____ _____.

Ayaka: I'm so envious*! I plan to (9)_____ to Europe while I'm still in college. But I've got to* save some money for that! That's why I have a part-time job.

John:　Are you (10)_____ to your part-time job again today?

Ayaka: Yes, absolutely*!

> * Versailles ヴェルサイユ（フランス・パリ郊外の街、ルイ14世とマリーアントワネットが住んだ宮殿がある）
>   envious うらやましい　have got to しなければならない　absolutely まったくその通り

Questions: Work with a partner. Take turns asking and answering the questions below about **Conversation 1**. Answer **in full sentences** and write the answers on the lines.　ペアで行います。Conversation 1の会話について、下の質問をし、答えを書き取りましょう。答えるときは、単語ではなく文章（主語・述語がはいった文）で答えること。1人だけが聞いたり1人だけが答えたりするのではなく、交互に質問し、2人とも全ての質問をし、全ての質問に答えるようにすること。

1. Has John been to France before?

   _____

2. Why has he been there so often?

   _____

3. Why does Ayaka want to visit Paris?

   _____

4. How many times has John been to Versailles?

   _____

5. When does Ayaka plan to go to Europe?

   _____

6. How is Ayaka saving money for her trip?

   _____

Practice: With a partner, write a conversation based on **Conversation 1**. Fill in the blanks below with information about yourselves. Take turns reading your conversation out loud, changing roles each time. パートナーと協力して空欄を埋め、自分たちに関するオリジナル会話文を作りましょう。書き終えたら声に出して2度練習します。大きくはっきりとした声で読み上げること。2度目は役を交代して読み上げましょう。

A: _____, have you ever been to _____?

B: Yes, I've been to _____.

A: That's nice! I would love to visit _____. I've never been there.

B: There is a lot to see in _____. What would you like to do most there?

A: I'd like to _____.

B: I've _____. It was one of the best _____ I've ever _____.

A: I'm so envious! I hope to _____ while I am still in college. I've got to save some money for that!

B: Is that why you are _____?

A: Yes, absolutely!

II. Grammar & Practice: **Present perfect** 現在完了形

Read the **Appendix** on page 114 (Unit 9 Present Perfect) and look at the explanation below. To express experiences that you have had, you often need to use the present-perfect tense (have + past participle):
付録 114 ページ「現在完了形」の説明と下記の説明をよく読みましょう。現在までの経験について話す時は現在完了形を用います。

> I **have visited** London.
>
> He **has eaten** Vietnamese food.

Such expressions are often followed by "*before*" or by the *number of times* you have had the experience:
経験の現在完了形は "before" や経験数（once, twice, three times…）と共に用いることがよくあります。

> I **have visited** London *before*.
>
> He **has eaten** Vietnamese food *three times*.

Such expressions are also used with "*never*" or "*ever*" to make negative sentences and questions:
"never" や "ever" とともに用いることも多いです：

> **Have** you *ever* **made** lasagna?
>
> She **has** *never* **seen** a horror movie.

Note: You cannot use the present-perfect tense with a specific period of time. In such cases, use the simple past tense: 現在完了形は特定の時間を示す語句とは一緒に使えません。過去の特定の時間に何かをしたと言いたい場合は過去形を使いましょう。

> I **went** to London **last year**.
>
> I **ate** shaved ice* **when I was in Hawaii**.

* shaved ice かき氷

Exercise 1: Write the past-participle forms of the verbs below and read them out to your partner. Note that some verbs are **regular** and some are **irregular**. 下の表の動詞の過去分詞形を書き込んでください。その後パートナーに向かってひとつひとつ読み上げましょう。不規則変化する動詞もあるので気を付けてください。

visit		read		drink	
do		make		take	
see		write		go	
play		watch		live	
buy		hear		work	
wear		be		meet	
climb		eat		draw	

Exercise 2: With a partner, take turns asking each other questions about your experiences using the "Have you ever …?" pattern. Make up your questions using the hints/topics in the boxes below and the verb past participles you wrote in the chart in **Exercise 1**. Get additional information from your partner by asking follow-up questions such as *When did you …? Who did you …? OR How many times …?*

ペアで行います。"Have you ever...?" を使い、相手に経験の有無を尋ねてください。Exercise 1 で変化させた動詞を使います。経験の有無をきいたらもう少し詳しく聞いてみましょう。その時は過去形を使って尋ねましょう。例えば、"When did you...?" "Who did you...?" "How many times...?" などを使います。下の例を参考にしてください。経験の有無を答える時は "before" や "never"、または回数表現（once, twice, three times...）も使ってみてください。質問は二人称で、パートナーの答えは三人称で書き入れてください。

Follow this example:

    Say: *"Have you ever been to Kyoto" "Yes, I have."*

             "When did you go there?" "I went there last year with a friend."

    Write: *Yes, he/she has been to Kyoto once. He/She went there last year with a friend.*

             (OR: No, he/she has never been to Kyoto.)

ペアで行います。下記の表の中にある言葉を用いて、経験を聞く質問文を作りましょう。1 を 1 人が作ったら、その次の質問はもう 1 人が作る、というように順番にやりましょう。「今までに」を意味する "ever" も使ってみてください。お互いに質問をし合い、聞かれた方は同じく現在完了を使って答えます。答える時は、「before」「never」または回数も使いましょう。そして聞きながら相手の回答を三人称で書き留めます。（"He has been to Kyoto twice." など。）

1. brass-band music	(Question:)
(Partner's answer:)	
2. an Indian movie	
3. Nara	
4. a book by a foreign writer	
5. strong medicine	
6. as a tutor	
7. a mountain	
8. a professional baseball game	

9. Coca-Cola Zero	
10. a birthday cake	
11. badminton	
12. Thai food	
13. a Halloween costume	
14. a love letter	
15. a famous person	
16. in Tokyo	
17. a self-portrait	
18. up Tokyo Skytree	
19. something very expensive	
20. part-time work	

III. Conversation 2

Listen to the conversation below. Then take turns practicing it with a partner, changing roles each time.
会話を聞き、パートナーと一緒に練習しましょう。1度読み終えたら役を交代してもう1度練習します。

Ayaka and John talk again after class.　アヤカとジョンは授業後にまた話をしています。 19

John:　It's been a long day! I feel a little tired, but I'd like to go to the gym. I need some exercise.

Ayaka:　Me, too. What do you usually do there?

John:　I usually run for half an hour and also do some weight training.

Ayaka:　Sounds like a good workout.

John:　I'd like to try some martial arts, though. Have you ever tried martial arts?

Ayaka:　Yeah. I've done aikido before.

John:　Cool! Did you like it?

Ayaka:　It was OK, but it was quite difficult. I liked yoga better. I've gone to local yoga classes a couple of times.

John:　You should keep it up. They say it's good for you.

Ayaka:　I know. I think I will go again this weekend.

Practice: With a partner, write a conversation based on **Conversation 2**. Fill in the blanks below with information about yourselves. Take turns reading your conversation out loud, changing roles each time.
パートナーと協力し、上の Conversation 2 をもとに、自分たちに関するオリジナル会話文を作成しましょう。書き終えたら声に出して2度練習します。大きくはっきりとした声で読み上げること。2度目は役を交代して読み上げましょう。

A:　It's been a long day! I feel a little tired, but I'd like to go to _____. I need _____.

B:　Me, too. What do you usually _____ there?

A:　I usually _____.

B:　It sounds _____.

A:　But tonight, I'd like to _____. Have you ever tried _____?

B:　_____. I've _____ before.

A:　_____! Did you _____?

B:　I learned _____. _____, but

_____. I _____ better. I've

_____.

A:　I often _____ to _____. _____ is good for you.

B:　You're right. I think I will _____. Would you like to

_____?

IV. Active Learning

With a partner, make up ten questions about experiences to ask the other members of your class. For questions 1-5 (see below), use the standard "Have you ever …?" sentence pattern. For questions 1A-5A, to get more information, make up follow-up questions using "How many times …?" OR "Who did you …?" OR "When did you …?" Write your questions under **Questions** below. After you finish writing, walk around the class and ask your classmate your questions. When you find someone who answers "Yes, I have …" to a question, ask him/her your follow-up question. Write his/her answers under **Answers** below. Follow this Example:

例：   * *Have you ever played golf? Nori has played golf before.*

     ** *When did you play golf? He played it in high school with his classmate.*

ペアで行います。ペアの相手以外のクラスメートに経験を尋ねるための質問を 10 個作りましょう。1Q 〜 5Q までは "Have you ever...?" を使います。1A 〜 5A の質問はもう少し詳しく聞くための質問です。"How many times...?"（何度〜しましたか）"Who did you...?"（誰と〜しましたか）"When did you...?"（いつ〜しましたか）などを使ってください。質問は下の表の左側に書き込みましょう。書き終えたら、教室を歩いてクラスメートに質問してください。"Yes, I have..." と答えたクラスメートがいたら、もう少し詳しい質問（1A 〜 5A）をして、全ての答えを表の右側に書き入れてください。上の例を参考に進めましょう。

Questions: **Answers:**

1. Q:	A:
1A.	
2. Q:	A:
2A.	
3. Q:	A:
3A.	
4. Q:	A:
4A.	
5. Q:	A:
5A.	

● **Review Game**

Work with a group, but use only one book. Follow these instructions:
下記の 1 ～ 4 の指示に従い、グループで行います。教科書は 1 冊だけ使って構いません。(コインが必要です)

1. Use a small object such as an eraser or a piece of paper as a marker.
    消しゴムや付箋のような小さなものを 1 つ用意してください。駒として使います。

2. Play "rock, paper, scissors" to decide who goes first. Take turns moving your marker.
    ジャンケンをして順番を決めます。表の 1 から順に交代で進めます。

3. Each player takes a turn by flipping a coin. If the coin lands face up, move two spaces. If the coin lands tails up, move one space.
    各プレイヤーが交代でコインを投げます。コインが表の場合は 2 つ進めてください。コインが裏の場合は 1 つしか進めません。

4. When you land on a space, ask and answer the question on it. Answer **in a full sentence**.
    とまったマスの質問を読み上げて、正しい英文で答えましょう。

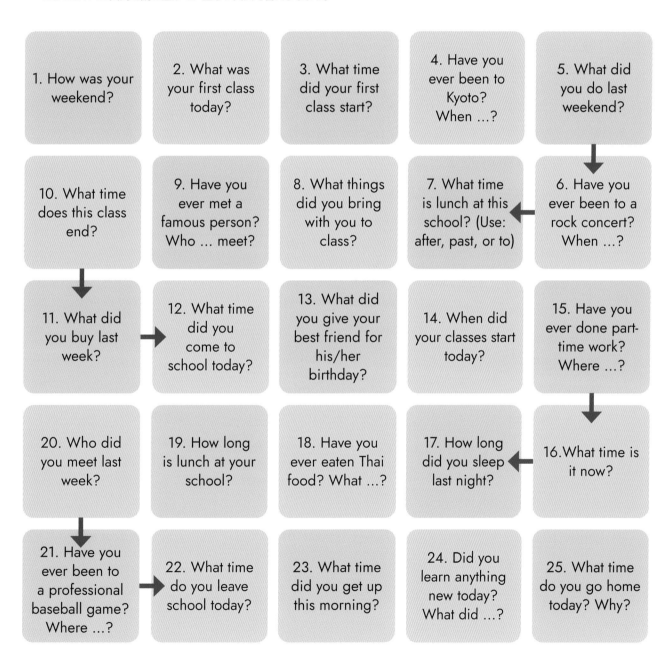

1. How was your weekend?

2. What was your first class today?

3. What time did your first class start?

4. Have you ever been to Kyoto? When …?

5. What did you do last weekend?

10. What time does this class end?

9. Have you ever met a famous person? Who … meet?

8. What things did you bring with you to class?

7. What time is lunch at this school? (Use: after, past, or to)

6. Have you ever been to a rock concert? When …?

11. What did you buy last week?

12. What time did you come to school today?

13. What did you give your best friend for his/her birthday?

14. When did your classes start today?

15. Have you ever done part-time work? Where …?

20. Who did you meet last week?

19. How long is lunch at your school?

18. Have you ever eaten Thai food? What …?

17. How long did you sleep last night?

16. What time is it now?

21. Have you ever been to a professional baseball game? Where …?

22. What time do you leave school today?

23. What time did you get up this morning?

24. Did you learn anything new today? What did …?

25. What time do you go home today? Why?

Part A: Work with partner. As you take turns reading sentences below out loud, fill in the blanks with the appropriate forms of the verbs in parentheses or with the correct times. Spell out the times indicated in the parentheses. ペアで行います。1〜20 の文章を交代で読み上げながら下線部を埋めていきましょう。下線部には（　　）内の動詞を適切な形にして入れるか、（　　）内の時間を文字におこして入れましょう。

1. "What did you _____(buy) at the convenience store?"

   "I _____(buy) something to drink."

2. John usually eats dinner at _____(7:45). [Use "to."]

3. She _____(take) strong medicine before. She didn't like it.

4. Mary _____(go) to Europe many times.

5. She _____(go) there last summer.

6. The movie starts at _____(2:30). [Use "past."]

7. I _____(make) a birthday cake for a friend before.

8. Kim _____(study) for her test for many hours last night.

9. I usually start studying at _____(8:15). [Use "after."]

10. When did you _____(climb) Mt. Fuji?

11. I _____(climb) Mt. Fuji in August.

12. What time is it? It's _____(1:05).
    [Write both the formal and conversational ways.]

13. I have _____(read) the book, but I haven't _____(write) my report.

14. We _____(see) the new Star Wars movie on Saturday.

15. Second period starts at _____(10:40) and ends at _____(12:10).

16. Jenny just _____(hear) loud music coming from the next room.

17. "Have you ever _____(be) to Mexico?" "I _____(go) there in 2016."

18. I _____(get) sick last week. I _____(have) a cold.

19. I _____(have) influenza two times. The last time I _____(have) it _____(be) last year.

20. John _____ never _____(eat) osechi, Japan's special New Year's food.

Part B: Find someone who … With a partner, make up six questions about experiences to ask the other members of your class. Write your questions based on the hints in 1-6 below using the "Have you ever …? sentence pattern in the parentheses. After you finish writing, walk around the class and ask your classmates your questions. When you find someone who answers "Yes, I have …" to a question, write the person's name on the "Name" line. Then, to learn more about him/her, ask a follow-up question (When, Who with, What, etc.). Write his/her answer on lines after "More information." ペアで行います。ペアの相手と一緒に、ペアの相手以外のクラスメートに尋ねる 6 個の質問を考えましょう。1 ～ 6 の語句にある経験をしたことがあるかどうかを "Have you ever...?" を使って聞きます。書き終えたら、教室内を歩いてクラスメートに質問してください。"Yes, I have..." と答えた学生がいたら、彼／彼女の名前を "Name" の下線部に英語で書き込んでください。それからもう少し詳しく聞いてみましょう（例えば、いつ、だれと、何を、どこでしたか、など）。その答えは三人称を用いて "More information" と書かれた下線部に書いてください。

1. go bowling

   (Have you ever …?) _____

   Name: _____

   More information: _____

2. be to a foreign country

   (Have you ever …?) _____

   Name: _____

   More information: _____

3. eat Vietnamese food

   (Have you ever …?) _____

   Name: _____

   More information: _____

4. buy alcoholic drinks/beverages

   (Have you ever …?) _____

   Name: _____

   More information: _____

5. take an English writing class

   (Have you ever …?) _____

   Name: _____

   More information: _____

6. wear a suit

   (Have you ever …?) _____

   Name: _____

   More information: _____

Unit 10

Can I ask you a favor?

Auxiliary Verbs

I. Conversation 1

As you listen to the conversation below, fill in the missing parts. Check your answers with a partner and with your teacher. Repeat each line after your teacher, and then take turns practicing the conversation with your partner, changing roles each time. 会話を聞き、下の会話文の下線部を埋めましょう。パートナーと答えを確認してください。そのあと、先生と答え合わせをし、先生に続いて文を復唱してください。最後にパートナーと会話を練習しましょう。1度読み終えたら次は役を交代してもう1度行いましょう。

John asks Ayaka for a favor*.
ジョンは休んでしまった授業の配布物をコピーさせて欲しいとアヤカに頼んでいます。

🎧20

John:　Hi, Ayaka. (1)_____ I ask you a favor?

Ayaka:　Sure, hi, John. You were absent (2)_____ Art class this morning. What happened?

John:　Well, the train didn't come on time, so I (3)_____ make it* to first period. So,

(4)_____ I borrow* the handouts from the class, if there are any?

Ayaka:　Sure. Here they are, and we (5)_____ an assignment* for next week.

John:　Thanks. What's the assignment?

Ayaka:　We (6)_____ _____ go to a museum and then, after we get home, make a rough* drawing of something we remembered.

John:　What?! From memory? That (7)_____ be really hard to do! What museum

(8)_____ I go to?

Ayaka:　Any museum is OK. The assignment (9)_____ be hard, but it (10)_____ be interesting, too.

* favor 親切な行為　make it 間に合う　borrow 借りる　assignment 宿題　rough 大まかな

Questions: Work with a partner. Take turns asking and answering the questions below about **Conversation 1**. Answer **in full sentences** and write the answers on the lines. ペアで行います。Conversation 1の会話について、下の質問をし、答えを書き取りましょう。答えるときは、単語ではなく文章（主語・述語がはいった文）で答えること。1人だけが聞いたり1人だけが答えたりするのではなく、交互に質問し、2人とも全ての質問をし、全ての質問に答えるようにすること。

1. What class was John absent from?

    _____

2. Why couldn't John make it to first period?

    _____

3. What did John ask to borrow from Ayaka?

    _____

4. What is the assignment?

    _____

    _____

5. What does John think about the assignment?

    _____

Practice: With a partner, write a conversation based on **Conversation 1**. Fill in the blanks below with information about yourselves. Take turns reading your conversation out loud, changing roles each time. パートナーと協力して空欄を埋め、自分たちに関するオリジナル会話文を作りましょう。書き終えたら声に出して2度練習します。大きくはっきりとした声で読み上げること。2度目は役を交代して読み上げましょう。

A: Hi, _____. Can I ask you a favor?

B: Sure, _____. What happened? You were absent from _____ class

    _____.

A: Well, _____, so I couldn't make it to _____ period. May I borrow the handouts from the class, if there are any?

B: Sure. Here are the handouts, and we have an assignment for _____.

A: Thanks. What's the assignment?

B: We _____.

A: What? _____? That will be really hard to do!

B: Yes, it could be, but _____.

II. Grammar & Practice: Auxiliary Verbs 助動詞

Read about auxiliary verbs in the chart below and on page 115 of the **Appendix** (Unit 10 Auxiliary Verbs).
付録 115 ページの「助動詞」の説明と下の表をよく読んでください。

Auxiliary verbs（助動詞）	Japanese	Examples
can/can't	～することができる／できない ～してもよい	She **can** sing well. / I **can't** play the piano. **Can** I have a cookie? / You **can't** go shopping today.
could/couldn't	～することができた／できなかった ～していただけますか［could you ～?］	He **could** (was able to) swim when he was only three years old. / I **couldn't** help him yesterday. **Could** you help me with my homework?
may/may not	～するかもしれない［50% chance］ ～してもよい／～してはいけない	It **may** rain later. **May** I sit here? You **may not** smoke here.
might/might not	～かもしれない／しないかもしれない ［20 ～ 30 ％の確率］	The weather **might** get better soon. I **might not** finish my report on time.
have to (must)/ don't have to	～しなければならない ～しなくてもよろしい	You **have to** (**must**) go to school until the end of junior high school. ("Must" is usually used to talk about strict orders, rules, or laws.) You **don't have to** go to high school, but most do.
shall/(shall not)	～しましょうか	**Shall I** carry that for you? **Shall we** go out to dinner?
should/shouldn't/ ought to/ought not to	～するべきである／～するべきではない ～して当然だ／～するべきではない	We **should/ought to** study for the test tonight. You **shouldn't/ought not to** talk on your phone on the train. We **ought to** look at the timetable* at the station.
will/won't	～する（つもりである）［意志］／ ～しない（つもりである） ～するだろう	I'**ll** meet you later. / We **won't** go to Disneyland tomorrow, because it **will** (is going to) rain.
would/wouldn't	～するかもしれない／～しないかもしれない ～するだろう ～したい／したくない（would like ～／ wouldn't like ～）	It **would/wouldn't** be fun to live in a foreign country. He **would** go to London, if he could. I **would like** a cup of coffee, please. / I **wouldn't like** to work all night.

* timetable 時刻表

Exercise 1: Work with a partner. Fill in the blank in each sentence below with one of the auxiliary verb forms in the chart above. Then take turns asking each other the questions. Write your partner's answers on the appropriate lines. ペアで行います。上の表の助動詞から適切なものを選び 1 ～ 10 の質問の下線部に書き込みましょう。ペアの相手と交代で質問し合い、相手の答えを "Partner's answer" の下線部に書いてください。

1. It _____ rain tomorrow. What do you think?

   Partner's answer: _____

2. _____ you like to have dinner with me tonight?

   Partner's answer: _____

3. _____ you ride a bicycle when you were five years old?

   Partner's answer: _____

4. Do you _____ take this class, or is it an elective*?

   Partner's answer: _____

5. Do you think I _____ get a tattoo?

   Partner's answer: _____

6. _____ we play video games tonight?

   Partner's answer: _____

7. _____ you be going on a trip soon?

   Partner's answer: _____

8. _____ you ski?

   Partner's answer: _____

9. _____ I smoke here?

   Partner's answer: _____

10. _____ you drive a car?

    Partner's answer: _____

* elective 選択科目

Exercise 2: With a partner, fill in the blanks in the sentences below with auxiliary verbs from the chart on page 80. Some sentences take the negative form "not." Then take turns reading the completed sentences. ペアで行います。前のページの表にある助動詞から適切なものを選び 1 〜 10 の質問の下線部に書き込みましょう。否定形になる文には not(n't) を使いましょう。書き終えたら交代で完成文を読み上げましょう。

1. I'm sorry, I _____ go to your party tomorrow. I'm very busy.

2. You _____ finish your homework before you _____ watch TV.

3. It's hot in here. _____ I turn on the air conditioner?

4. _____ you like milk in your tea?

5. I _____ like to go to my grandparents' house in the country this summer, but I _____ study for the *Eiken*, so I probably _____ go.

6. It _____ be hot this summer, I'm sure!

7. John tried very hard, but he _____ finish his report in time. He _____ hand it in to the teacher a week late.

8. I _____ go to your apartment tomorrow and help you make the food for Ayaka's birthday party.

9. I really _____ go to bed earlier. I'm really tired these days.

10. All travelers from foreign countries _____ show their passports when they arrive at Narita Airport.

III. Conversation 2

Listen to the conversation below. Then take turns practicing it with a partner two times, changing roles each time. 会話を聞き、パートナーと一緒に練習しましょう。1度読み終えたら役を交代してもう1度練習します。

John and Ayaka talk about their Art assignment.
ジョンとアヤカが美術の課題について話しています。

21

John: So, Ayaka, what museum did you choose to visit for your assignment?

Ayaka: The other day, I went to The National Museum of Western Art in Ueno Park and made some drawings of Rodin's sculpture.

John: Wow, already? Good for you! I have to go to a museum this weekend, or I won't be able to hand in the assignment on time.

Ayaka: Where would you like to visit?

John: I am thinking of visiting the Edo-Tokyo Museum. What do you think?

Ayaka: Great idea! I've been there once, and there were many interesting displays. You really should go there while you are in Japan.

John: Thanks for the suggestion. But, may I ask you to come with me? I probably need somebody to translate and explain things.

Ayaka: Sure. Shall we have lunch, too? I know a good restaurant in the area.

John: Cool!

Practice: With a partner, write a conversation based on **Conversation 2**. Fill in the blanks below with information about yourselves. Take turns reading your conversation out loud, changing roles each time. パートナーと協力し、上の Conversation 2 をもとに、自分たちに関するオリジナル会話文を作成しましょう。書き終えたら声に出して2度練習します。大きくはっきりとした声で読み上げること。2度目は役を交代して読み上げましょう。

A: So, _____, what _____ did you choose to visit for your assignment?

B: The other day, I _____ and _____.

A: Wow, already? Great. I have to _____, or I won't be able to _____.

B: _____ would you like to _____?

A: I'm thinking of _____. What do you think?

B: Great idea! I _____. You _____ _____.

A: You're right! May I ask _____

B: Sure. Shall we _____?

A: _____.

IV. Active Learning

Exercise: Work with a partner. Make suggestions to him/her about what he/she should see or do in your hometown/home prefecture. Use the form "If you (go to …,), you (should/may/can/will/have to/could/might) …," as in these examples.　ペアで行います。ペアの相手に、あなたの出身地でするべきことやできるかもしれないこと、できること、するであろうこと、しなければならないこと（絶対したほうがよいこと）、してもよいかもしれないこと、などを言いましょう。"If you…, you should/may/can/will/have to/could/might…" を使います。下記の例を参考にしてください。

Examples:

"If you go to Kanagawa, you really **should** visit the aquarium."

"If you go to Yokohama, you **have to** try the *manju* in Chinatown."

"If you eat at Karyu Restaurant, you **might** want to eat dim sum."

"If you are thirsty, you **may** want to try bubble tea at Tapioca Tea Room."

"If you visit Yamashita Park, you **will** see many young couples enjoying the view."

Write what your partner suggests and your suggestions on the lines as you say them.　あなた自身の提案を "You" の部分の下線部に、パートナーが提案したことを "Your partner" の部分の下線部に記入していきましょう。

You:

Your prefecture: _____

_____

Your town/city: _____

_____

Your favorite restaurant: _____

_____

Your favorite shop: _____

_____

Your favorite park: _____

_____

Your partner:

Your partner's home prefecture: _____

_____

Your partner's home town/city: _____

_____

Your partner's favorite restaurant: _____

_____

Your partner's favorite shop: _____

_____

Your partner's favorite park: _____

_____

85

Unit 11

I'm going to visit my grandparents.

Future Tense

I. Conversation 1

As you listen to the conversation below, fill in the missing parts. Check your answers with a partner and with your teacher. Repeat each line after your teacher, and then take turns practicing the conversation with your partner, changing roles each time. 会話を聞き、下の会話文の下線部を埋めましょう。パートナーと答えを確認してください。そのあと、先生と答え合わせをし、先生に続いて文を復唱してください。最後にパートナーと会話を練習しましょう。1度読み終えたら次は役を交代してもう1度行いましょう。

John and Ayaka talk about their plans for their spring vacations.
ジョンとアヤカは春休みの計画について話しています。

🎧22

Ayaka: John, what are you (1)_____ during spring vacation?

John: I'm (2)_____ _____ visit Southeast Asia.

Ayaka: Wow! That sounds like fun. Which countries are you (3)_____ _____ _____ to?

John: I'm (4) _____ Vietnam, Cambodia, and Thailand.

Ayaka: Are you going (5)_____ the school's Travel Abroad program?

John: Yes, I am. I'll (6)_____ _____ with 25 other students. We all (7)_____ _____ volunteer while we are there.

Ayaka: How exciting! I'm (8)_____ going to visit my grandparents this spring.

John: Where do they (9)_____?

Ayaka: They live in Niigata, on the Japan Sea.

John: So, are you going to go to the (10)_____ while you're there?

Ayaka: I might, but it's still pretty cold there in March.

Questions: Work with a partner. Take turns asking and answering the questions below about **Conversation 1.** Answer **in full sentences** and write the answers on the lines. ペアで行います。Conversation 1の会話について、下の質問をし、答えを書き取りましょう。答えるときは、単語ではなく文章（主語・述語がはいった文）で答えること。1人だけが聞いたり1人だけが答えたりするのではなく、交互に質問し、2人とも全ての質問をし、全ての質問に答えるようにすること。

1. What's John doing during spring vacation?

   _____

2. What countries is he going to go to?

   _____

3. Who is he going with?

   _____

4. Where is Ayaka going this spring?

   _____

5. How is the beach in Niigata in the spring?

   _____

Practice: With a partner, write a conversation based on **Conversation 1.** Fill in the blanks below with information about yourselves. Take turns reading your conversation out loud, changing roles each time. パートナーと協力して空欄を埋め、自分たちに関するオリジナル会話文を作りましょう。書き終えたら声に出して2度練習します。大きくはっきりとした声で読み上げること。2度目は役を交代して読み上げましょう。

A: _____, what are you doing during spring vacation?

B: I'm _____.

A: That sounds _____. Which/What _____ are you going to

   _____?

B: I'm _____.

A: So, are you _____?

B: _____. I'll _____. What are you doing during spring vacation?

A: I'm _____.

B: Where _____?

A: _____.

B: _____?

A: _____.

II. Grammar & Practice: **Future Tense** 未来の表現

There are many ways to express the future tense in English. Study the different patterns below.

英語の未来の表現には様々なものがあります。付録 116 ページ「未来の表現」と下記をよく読み、様々な表現について、使い方やそれぞれの違いを理解しましょう。

1. **Simple present tense**: Used when you are talking about timetables and schedules.

   単純未来：時刻表や予定などを話す時に用いる。

   What time **does** the next train **leave**? / The next bus **doesn't leave** until 6 p.m. tonight.

   Class **starts** at 8:30 tomorrow morning.

   We **check in** after we arrive at the hotel

2. **Present continuous tense (be + ing)**: Used when you are talking about what you have already planned to do, or planned not to do, or what you are not planning to do in the near future.

   現在進行形：近い将来にすでにする（／しない）と決まっていることについて話すときに用いる。

   I'm **finishing** my report tonight.

   They're **coming** over to my place after school.

   She's **leaving** for New York on Monday.

   I'm **not going to** that rock festival.

3. **Be going to (do)**: Used when you are planning to do something in the future, or when you think something will or will not happen in the future.

   be going to 〜：なにかをする「つもり」のとき、なにかが起こる（起こらない）だろう、と言いたい時に用いる。

   We're **going to work** outside this weekend.

   I'm **going to visit** Paris after I graduate.

   It looks like it's **going to rain** this afternoon.

   He's **going to finish** his report tomorrow.

   I'm sad because I'm **not going to see** my favorite teacher again.

4. **Will (do)/won't (will not) do**: Used when you decide to do something at the time you are speaking, or when you have a strong will to do or not do something.

   will/won't: 今やろうと決めたことや、やる（やらない）意志を示す時に用いる。

   I'll **take out** the trash before I leave.

   (Ordering in a restaurant): I'll **have** the mixed pizza and oolong tea, please.

   Japan **will win** the World Cup next time for sure.

   I **will show** you where to find everything you need.

   Dan **won't** see his parents again until next year.

Exercise: Work with a partner. As you take turns reading the sentences below, fill in the most appropriate future-tense form of the verbs in parentheses. Some sentences are questions or negative and some can have more than one answer. For questions 11 and 12, make up two more statements about yourself using the future tense.　ペアで行います。1～12の文章を交代で読み上げながら、（　　）内の動詞を正しい未来表現に変えて書き込みましょう。質問文や否定文もあります。また、2つ以上の未来表現が使えるものもあります。11と12には未来表現を用いたオリジナル文を作って書き込みましょう。

1. What time _____ (do) the class finish today?

2. Waiter, I _____ (have) the spaghetti and meat sauce.

3. John _____ (play) tennis this weekend.

4. Who _____ (go) to a foreign country next summer?

5. Mary _____ (not leave) until morning.

6. Tom _____ (have) a big party for his next birthday.

7. I _____ (finish) my long report this Sunday, I'm sure.

8. What _____ (do) after this class?

9. _____ (eat) your box lunch in this classroom?

10. Don't worry. I _____ (not say) anything to him. I can keep a secret.

11. _____

12. _____

III. Conversation 2

Listen to the conversation below. Then take turns practicing it with a partner two times, changing roles each time.　会話を聞き、パートナーと一緒に練習しましょう。1 度読み終えたら役を交代してもう 1 度練習します。

Ayaka and John talk after class.　アヤカとジョンが授業の後に話をしています。 23

John:　What are you doing this weekend?

Ayaka:　I'm going to Disneyland with some friends. What are you doing?

John:　I'm not doing anything special. I'm just doing some homework and working on a report.

Ayaka:　That doesn't sound like much fun.

John:　But I am going to go to Disneyland in December when it's decorated for Christmas.

Ayaka:　It's beautiful then. There's not much going on between Halloween and Christmas.

John:　In America, we have Thanksgiving*. That's the day we eat turkey. This year I'm going to cook a turkey here in Japan.

Ayaka:　I've never had turkey before. May I come to your party?

John:　Of course. I'm inviting a few friends for a potluck*. What would you like to bring?

Ayaka:　I'll bring a pie for dessert.

John:　Great! Well, have a nice time at Disneyland.

* Thanksgiving（アメリカの）感謝祭　potluck 持ち寄りパーティ

Practice: With a partner, write a conversation based on **Conversation 2**. Fill in the blanks below with information about yourselves. Take turns reading your conversation out loud, changing roles each time.
パートナーと協力し、上の Conversation 2 をもとに、自分たちに関するオリジナル会話文を作成しましょう。書き終えたら声に出して 2 度練習します。大きくはっきりとした声で読み上げること。2 度目は役を交代して読み上げましょう。

A:　What are you doing this/next weekend?

B:　I'm _____. What are you doing?

A:　I'm _____.

B:　That _____.

A:　I'm _____.

B:　It's _____.

A:　Well, _____.

B:　I've _____.

　　Would you _____?

A:　Sure. I'd _____. _____?

B:　I'll _____.

A:　Great! I'm looking forward to it! Have a nice _____.

IV. Active Learning

With a partner, take turns asking and answering the questions below **in full sentences**. Write your partner's answers on the lines using the appropriate future-tense form.　ペアで行います。1〜10の質問を交代で読み上げ、それぞれ適切な未来表現を用いて答えましょう。相手の答えを下線部に書き込んでください。

1. What are you doing after class?

   _____

2. When are you going home tonight?

   _____

3. What are you going to do after you get home?

   _____

4. What time are you eating dinner tonight?

   _____

5. Where are you going this/next weekend?

   _____

6. What are you doing during your next long vacation?

   _____

7. When will you graduate from this school?

   _____

8. What are you going to do after you graduate?

   _____

9. What movie are you going to see next?

   _____

10. Who are you going to meet next week?

    _____

<table>
<tr><td>

Unit 12

</td><td>

I'm on the train.

Prepositions

</td></tr>
</table>

I. Conversation 1

As you listen to the conversation below, fill in the missing parts. Check your answers with a partner and with your teacher. Repeat each line after your teacher, and then take turns practicing the conversation with your partner, changing roles each time.　会話を聞き、下の会話文の下線部を埋めましょう。パートナーと答えを確認してください。そのあと、先生と答え合わせをし、先生に続いて文を復唱してください。最後にパートナーと会話を練習しましょう。1度読み終えたら次は役を交代してもう1度行いましょう。

Ayaka and John have arranged to meet for a movie and are talking on the phone.
アヤカとジョンは待ち合わせをしていて、電話で話しています。　🎧24

Ayaka:　Hi, John. Are you (1)_____ the station?

John:　No, I'm still (2)_____ the train, so I'll call you back (3)_____ I get off.

Ayaka:　OK, talk to you in a few minutes, then.

....

John:　Hi, again. Sorry I couldn't talk.

Ayaka:　It's quite all right. Where are you?

John:　I'm (4)_____ _____ _____ _____ the station. I'm not quite sure where I should be heading*.

Ayaka:　I'm at the café (5)_____ _____ a large bookshop. When you go out of the west gate, you will see a shopping mall (6)_____ _____ the station. Go (7)_____ the shopping mall all the way to the other end.

John:　Oh. Is it the café we ate (8)_____ before?

Ayaka:　That's right. But don't hurry. I have a book (9)_____ me, and the movie doesn't start until 2:20.

John:　Okay. I'll be there (10)_____ twenty minutes. I'm going to buy a new dictionary at the bookstore.

* be heading 向かっている

Questions: Work with a partner. Take turns asking and answering the questions below about **Conversation 1**. Answer **in full sentences** and write the answers on the lines. ペアで行います。Conversation 1の会話について、下の質問をし、答えを書き取りましょう。答えるときは、単語ではなく文章（主語・述語がはいった文）で答えること。1人だけが聞いたり1人だけが答えたりするのではなく、交互に質問し、2人とも全ての質問をし、全ての質問に答えるようにすること。

1. At the beginning of the conversation, is John at the station?

     _____

2. When will he call Ayaka back?

     _____

3. Where is Ayaka waiting?

     _____

4. Where is the café?

     _____

5. Why doesn't John have to hurry?

     _____

Practice: With a partner, write a conversation based on **Conversation 1**. Fill in the blanks below with information about yourselves. Take turns reading your conversation out loud, changing roles each time. パートナーと協力して空欄を埋め、自分たちに関するオリジナル会話文を作りましょう。書き終えたら声に出して2度練習します。大きくはっきりとした声で読み上げること。2度目は役を交代して読み上げましょう。

A: Hi, _____. Where are you?

B: I'm _____, so I will call you back _____.

A: OK, talk to you later.

     ⋯⋯⋯⋯⋯⋯⋯⋯⋯⋯⋯⋯⋯⋯⋯⋯⋯⋯⋯⋯⋯⋯⋯⋯

B: Hi, again. Sorry I couldn't talk.

A: It's quite all right. Where are you?

B: I'm _____. I'm not quite sure where I should be heading.

A: I'm at _____. When you _____, you will see _____

     _____. Go _____

     _____. I'll be waiting _____.

B: _____?

A: That's right. But don't hurry. I have a _____, and

     _____.

B: Okay. I'll be there in a few minutes. I need to use the restroom.

II. Grammar & Practice: Prepositions 前置詞

First, read the **Appendix** on page 117 (Unit 12 Prepositions) and look at the pictures below and on the next page. 付録117ページ「前置詞」をよく読み、下記Aと次ページBを見てください。

A. Prepositions of position 位置を表す前置詞

a. in

b. on

c. under

d. over

e. above

f. next to

g. behind

h. with

i. in front of

j. between

k. at (home)

l. across from

m. through

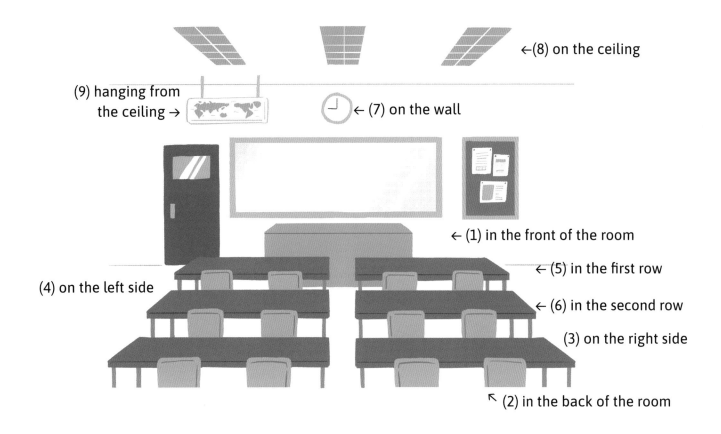

(8) on the ceiling

(9) hanging from the ceiling →

← (7) on the wall

← (1) in the front of the room

← (5) in the first row

(4) on the left side

← (6) in the second row

(3) on the right side

↖ (2) in the back of the room

B. Prepositions of time   時を表す前置詞

- **In → month, season**
  In January
  In (the) spring
  In two years

- **In → a future time**
  In five minutes
  In an hour

- **In → a particular year**
  In 1999
  In 2001

- **On → a particular day, date**
  On Tuesday   On May 7th
  On Saturday   On Monday morning
  On Christmas Day   On weekends

- **In → a particular time of day**
  In the morning
  In the afternoon
  In the evening
  (But: At noon, At night)

- **At → a particular time**
  At 8:00   At Christmas
  At 4:30 p.m.   At New Year's

- **Before → a particular time**
  Before school
  Before lunch

- **After → a particular time**
  After school
  After dinner

Exercise 1: Work with a partner. As you take turns reading the sentences below, fill in the blanks with the best preposition.　ペアで行います。1〜14 の各文を交代で読み上げながら下線部に入る適切な前置詞を考え、下線部に書きましょう。

1. I am sitting _____ a chair.

2. We are _____ school.

3. Our classes started again _____ September.

4. Our class always meets _____ Wednesday.

5. I usually sit _____ the back row.

6. The speakers are _____ the blackboard.

7. I always get hungry _____ lunch.

8. Classroom 201 is _____ this classroom. If we go out of this door and walk straight*, it's right there.

9. _____ school, I will go home.

10. First period starts _____ one o'clock.

11. We will graduate from this school _____ three years.

12. I dropped my eraser. It's _____ the desk.

13. Our class begins _____ 10:40.

14. The blackboard is _____ the front of the room.

* straight　まっすぐに

Exercise 2: Working with a partner, put the words in the box below in the correct columns.
ペアで行います。下のボックス内の各語句を、一緒に使うことができる前置詞の下の下線部に書きましょう。

6 o'clock	Wednesday afternoon	one hour
midnight	noon	summer
winter	Tuesday evening	September
Christmas Eve	Sunday morning	half past eleven
Saturday	1972	9 a.m.

IN

_____

_____

_____

_____

_____

AT

_____

_____

_____

_____

_____

ON

_____

_____

_____

_____

_____

III. Conversation 2

Listen to the conversation below. Then take turns practicing it with a partner two times, changing roles each time.　会話を聞き、パートナーと一緒に練習しましょう。1度読み終えたら役を交代してもう1度練習します。

Ayaka and John talk after the movie.　アヤカとジョンは映画を見た後に話をしています。 25

Ayaka:　So, John, what did you think of the movie?

John:　It was pretty good.

Ayaka:　I especially liked the part where he was riding on a rocket.

John:　Yeah, that was really funny. He got on the plane but ended up* on the rocket.

Ayaka:　But I wonder how he got through Security*.

John:　I don't know, but he got caught at the end.

Ayaka:　Oh, look at the time. I've got to go to my part-time job.

John:　When does it start?

Ayaka:　At five. I have to change clothes before I go.

John:　What time will you finish tonight?

Ayaka:　I get off work at nine.

John:　Since tomorrow is Sunday, do you want to have a late dinner tonight?

Ayaka:　Sure! Meet me in front of the convenience store at five after nine. There's a really good ramen shop next door.

* end up 結局は〜になる　Security 警備

Practice: With a partner, write a conversation based on **Conversation 2**. Fill in the blanks below with information about yourselves. Take turns reading your conversation out loud, changing roles each time.
パートナーと協力し、上の Conversation 2 をもとに、自分たちに関するオリジナル会話文を作成しましょう。書き終えたら声に出して2度練習します。大きくはっきりとした声で読み上げること。2度目は役を交代して読み上げましょう。

A:　So, what did you think of _____?

B:　It _____.

A:　I liked _____.

B:　_____.

A:　_____.

B:　_____.

A:　When _____?

B:　_____. _____?

A:　_____.

B:　_____!

IV. Active Learning

With a partner, take turns asking and answering the questions below. Write each other's answers on the lines **in full sentences**. Make sure you use the correct prepositions.　ペアで行います。1 ～ 10 の質問を交代で読み上げ、単語ではなく文章にして答えましょう。お互いの答えを下線部に書きましょう（三人称を用いた文章で書いてください）。

1. Where were you at 8 a.m. this morning?

    _____

2. Where is your best friend now?

    _____

3. Where's the blackboard in this room?

    _____

4. Where are you sitting?

    _____

5. Where is the teacher right now?

    _____

6. When is your next test?

    _____

7. When is your next meal*?

    _____

8. When is your next report due*?

    _____

9. When is your next class?

    _____

10. When does your next vacation start?

    _____

* meal 食事　due 期限が来る

● **Review Game**

Work with a group, but use only one book. Follow these instructions:
下記の1～4の指示に従い、グループで行います。教科書は1冊だけ使って構いません。（コインが必要です）

1. Use a small object such as an eraser or a piece of paper as a marker.
   消しゴムや付箋のような小さなものを1つ用意してください。駒として使います。

2. Play "rock, paper, scissors" to decide who goes first. Take turns moving your marker.
   ジャンケンをして順番を決めます。表の1から順に交代で進めます。

3. Each player takes a turn by flipping a coin. If the coin lands face up, move two spaces. If the coin lands tails up, move one space.
   各プレイヤーが交代でコインを投げます。コインが表の場合は2つ進めてください。コインが裏の場合は1つしか進めません。

4. When you land on a space, ask and answer the question on it. Answer **in a full sentence**.
   とまったマスの質問を読み上げて、正しい英文で答えましょう。

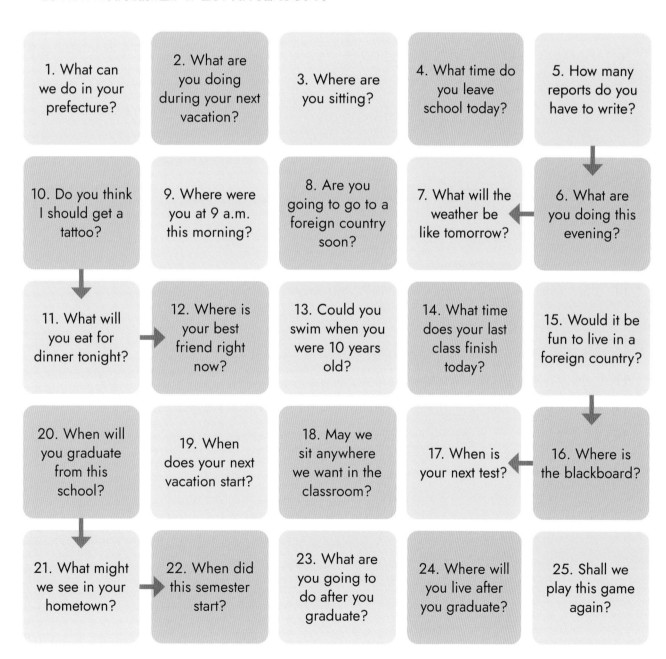

1. What can we do in your prefecture?

2. What are you doing during your next vacation?

3. Where are you sitting?

4. What time do you leave school today?

5. How many reports do you have to write?

10. Do you think I should get a tattoo?

9. Where were you at 9 a.m. this morning?

8. Are you going to go to a foreign country soon?

7. What will the weather be like tomorrow?

6. What are you doing this evening?

11. What will you eat for dinner tonight?

12. Where is your best friend right now?

13. Could you swim when you were 10 years old?

14. What time does your last class finish today?

15. Would it be fun to live in a foreign country?

20. When will you graduate from this school?

19. When does your next vacation start?

18. May we sit anywhere we want in the classroom?

17. When is your next test?

16. Where is the blackboard?

21. What might we see in your hometown?

22. When did this semester start?

23. What are you going to do after you graduate?

24. Where will you live after you graduate?

25. Shall we play this game again?

Part A: Work with a partner. As you take turns reading the sentences below, fill in the blanks with the most appropriate word or words.   ペアで行います。1〜20 の下線部に正しい語句を入れながら、各文を交代で読み上げましょう。

1. "_____ you like to eat dinner with me tonight?"

   "Sure. Where _____ we eat?"

2. _____ you drive a car? I'm surprised. I thought you _____.

3. John _____ NBA basketball on TV this weekend.

4. Mary _____ leave until tomorrow morning.

5. _____ school, I'm _____ home.

6. It looks like it's _____ rain soon.

7. The restrooms are _____ this classroom.

8. I'm _____ a big party for my next birthday.

9. _____ I smoke in this room?

10. My friend just arrived _____ Tokyo Station.

11. _____ two years, I _____ graduate from this school.

12. _____ you go to your grandparents house next vacation?

13. _____ New Year's, we usually eat *osechi*.

14. Don't worry. I _____ tell him your secret.

15. We are _____ the classroom now.

16. Christmas is _____ December, _____ December 25th.

17. _____ you play tennis?

18. I usually go to bed _____ midnight.

19. I _____ finish my report this weekend, I'm sure.

20. I _____ study hard for my test.

Part B: With a partner, take turns asking and answering the questions below. Write your partner's answers on the lines **in full sentences**.　ペアで行います。交代で相手に 1 〜 10 の質問をします。相手の言った答えを下線部に書き込みましょう。**文章にして書き込むこと。**

1. When you enter a foreign country, what do you have to do?

    _____

2. What are you going to do during your next vacation?

    _____

3. Shall we have dinner together tonight?

    _____

4. What are you doing after class?

    _____

5. When is your next class?

    _____

6. What should you do tonight?

    _____

7. What are you going to do after you get home tonight?

    _____

8. When does this semester end?

    _____

9. What will you do after you graduate from this school?

    _____

10. On what day do we have English class?

    _____

Appendix

0. Parts of Speech
品　詞

英語にはそれぞれ役割の異なる 8 種類の詞＝ 8 品詞があります。

名詞　物事やひとの名前

例）物質名詞→ apple, desk, pen, notebook, classroom, man, woman, child など
抽象名詞→ freedom, information, necessity など
集合名詞→ people, family など
固有名詞→ Japan, Murakami など

代名詞　名詞の代わりに使うもの

例）人称代名詞（わたし、彼、彼女、あなた、私たち、彼らなど）：I, you, he, she, we, they
所有代名詞：（「〜のもの」を意味）mine, yours, his, hers, ours, theirs
再帰代名詞：（「〜自身」）myself, yourself, himself, herself, ourselves, themselves
指示代名詞：（これ、それ、あれ、これら、それら、あれら、そういう〜、など）this, that, these, those, such
疑問代名詞（疑問詞）：（何、どちら、誰など名詞を尋ねるとき）what, which, who
不定代名詞：（指示する名詞を特定しない）another, some, one, none, somebody など

		〜は、〜が	〜の	〜を、〜に	〜のもの
単数形	1 人称	I	my	me	mine
	2 人称	you	your	you	yours
	3 人称 （男）	he	his	him	his
	（女）	she	her	her	hers
	それ	it	its	it	its
複数形	1 人称	we	our	us	ours
	2 人称	you	your	you	yours
	3 人称	they	their	them	theirs

動詞　動作や状態をあらわす語

1）be 動詞と一般動詞
be 動詞は主語によって、is, are, am, 時制によって was, were, being, been などに変化します。
一般動詞：be 動詞以外の動詞すべてをさします。

2）動作動詞と状態動詞（active/static）
動詞には、動作（〜する）を表す動詞と、状態（〜である、〜している）を表す動詞があります。
例）I walk to school every day. →「歩く」動作
I eat my lunch at noon every day. →「食べる」動作
I am a student. →「〜である」状態（先ほどの Be 動詞は状態動詞の一つです）
I have some money. →「持っている」状態

＊　その他の状態動詞の例：live, know, like, love, stand, belong, believe

＊　状態動詞は日本語では「〜している」と表現することも多いですが、一時的な状態を除いては進行形（be 〜 ing）にはなりません。例えば「私は赤いペンを持っている（所有）」は I am having a red pen ではなく、I have a red pen. です

＊　動作なのか状態なのかに迷ったら、その行為を一旦やめてまたすぐに（例えば 5 秒後に）再開できるかどうか、と考えてみましょう。やめられなかったら状態だと考えます。（例：「住んでいる」→一旦やめて 5 秒後に再開できることではない）⇒ I live ...

3）　自動詞・他動詞の区別

自動詞 (Vi)：　動作が他人やものに及ばない（走る、歩く、寝るなど）＝目的語をとらない

他動詞 (Vt)：　動作が他人やものに及ぶ（「〜を…する」〜をとる、〜を作る、〜を愛する、など）＝目的語をとる

同じ動詞でも自動詞として使われたり他動詞として使われたりする場合もあります。

例）　I run fast.「私は速く走る（＝私は走るのが速い）」（自動詞としての run）

　　　I run a company.「私は会社を経営する（している）」（他動詞としての run）

辞書にはある単語が自動詞か他動詞か、他動詞の時の意味、自動詞の時の意味が書いてあります。日本語で「〜を」と表現しない場合でも英語では他動詞の場合があります。（例：「〜について議論する」の discuss は他動詞です。つまり discuss about 〜ではなく、discuss 〜と直接目的語をとります。また反対に日本語では「〜を」と表現する場合でも英語では自動詞のこと（目的語をとらない）があります（例：I thought about her.「彼女のことを考えた」He waited for me. 彼は私を待っていてくれた。）

4）　活用

動詞は

・人称（わたし、あなた、彼、彼女、彼ら、それら）

・時制（過去形、過去分詞形など）

によって語形が変化します。

「3・単・現の "s"」

形容詞　名詞・代名詞を修飾する（「どんな〜」にあたる部分）。冠詞等の限定詞もここに含まれる。

副詞　動詞・形容詞・他の副詞を修飾する

前置詞　名詞・代名詞の前において句をつくり、句全体として一つの品詞の役割をするもの

接続詞　語と語、句と句、節と節を接続するもの

間投詞　呼びかけや感情をあらわす言葉（「あ！」「ええと」「まあ」など）

Unit 1 Subject-Verb Agreement
主語と動詞の一致

英語では、主語によって動詞の形が変わります。主語に一致する動詞の変化を見て行きましょう。

Present Tense（現在形）

Singular（単数）:

私	I am/speak
あなた	You are/speak
彼・彼女・それ	He/She/It is/speaks

Plural（複数）:

私たち	We are/speak
あなたたち	You are/speak
彼ら・それら	They are/speak

Past Tense（過去形）: 主語が単数か複数かによって、Be 動詞が変化します。

Singular（単数）:

私	I was
あなた	You were
彼・彼女・それ	He/She/It was

Plural（複数）:

私たち	We were
あなたたち	You were
彼ら・それら	They were

Spelling（verbs after He/She/It）三単現の S

三人称（「私」「あなた」以外）で単数の場合（彼・彼女・それ・単数の名詞）は、動詞の現在形の原型が以下のように変化します。

-s	buys, thinks, comes, plays, takes
-es	(after: ch, o, sh, s, ss, z) watches, washes, goes, misses
-ies	(after: consonant［子音］+ y) studies, cries,

「every」と「each」は三人称単数として使います。

Every and each are 3rd person singular.

Everyone is ...	（× Everyone are）
Everybody gets ...	（× Everybody get）
Each person wins ...	（× Each person win）
Everything does ...	（× Everything do）

Unit 2 Be Verbs & Do Verbs
Be 動詞と一般動詞

英語には大きく分けて 2 種類の動詞があります：「Be 動詞」と「一般動詞」です。

Be 動詞　Be 動詞は、主語が「どういう状態にあるか」を表すときに使います。

　　　　　例えば、I am happy という文の主語の I は、「幸せな状態 = happy」にあります。

　　　　　また、He is a student という文の主語の He は、「学生 a student である」という状態です。

　　　　　主語が女性でも同じく is、主語が We や You や They なら使われる Be 動詞は Are です。

一般動詞　一般動詞は、主語が「何をするか（しているか）」を表すとき使います。（本教科書では一般動詞のこと
　　　　　を英語で Do Verb と読んでいます。）

　　　　　　例えば、I go to a school　という文では、「（学校に）行く」という「何をするか」が示されます。

※一般動詞の二つの種類

　一般動詞には、さらに 2 つの種類があります：「自動詞」と「他動詞」です。

【自動詞】　自動詞は、その文のなかで、「対象物」がないこと、つまり動作が及ぶ相手がいない場合です。

　　　　　I sleep「私は眠る」という文では、「〜をどうする」という意味合いはありません。あくまでも「私が〜する」
　　　　　です。これを自動詞といいます。

【他動詞】　他動詞は、反対に、動作が及ぶ対象がある場合です。

　　　　　I see you every day「私はあなたに毎日会う」という文では、「会う」という行為に「あなた」という
　　　　　対象がいます。

　　　　　他動詞では、原則として、動詞のすぐ後に対象物（名詞）がきます。前置詞などがくる場合は、自動詞です：
　　　　　I look at you「私はあなたを見る」⇒ look は自動詞です。

● Be 動詞文を疑問文にしたいときは、Am/Are/Is/Was/Were をまずおき、次に主語、補語（形容詞や名詞）
　を続けて、必要に応じて、場所や時などの表現を付けた後に「？」を付けます。
　► He is hungry 彼はお腹がすいている → Is he hungry?　彼はお腹がすいていますか。

● 一般動詞文を疑問文にしたいときは、まず Do/Does/Did をつけます。その後に主語を置き、動詞の原形を
　続け、目的語（対象物）や必要に応じて、場所、時などの表現を付けた後に、「？」をつけます。
　► She likes pizza. 彼女はピザが好きです → Does she like pizza?　彼女はピザが好きですか。

Units 3&4
Countable & Uncountable Nouns
数えられる名詞と数えられない名詞

英語の名詞には、1つの〜、2つの〜、と数えられる名詞と、数えられない名詞があります。

数えられる名詞の特徴

- 1, 2, 3 と数え、2つ以上の場合は語尾に s/es をつける：a (one) dog, two dogs ...
- 複数形がある（s/es を語尾に。もしくは不規則変化する）：dogs, cats, wolf → wolves, foot → feet
- "How many" を使って数をたずねる
- "not many 〜" をつけて、あまり多くないことを表現する
- "There are 〜s" という形で、「〜がある」と表現する
- "a lot of 〜s" という形で、「〜がたくさん」と表現する
- "some 〜s" "a few of 〜s" で、「少しの・2、3の〜」と表現する
- 1つのものに言及するときは、冠詞の a をつけて表現する

数えられない名詞の特徴

（数えられないとは：1、2、3、と数えないもの。a や語尾の s がつかない）

- 液体　粒状のもの、抽象的なもの、集合名詞（「りんご」は数えられるが、「果物」は数えない）、原料・材料・生地、溶けるもの（アイスクリーム等）などは数えない。
- 複数形にならない（従って語尾に s や es をつけない）
- "How much" を使って、量をたずねる
- "not much" をつけてあまり多くないことを表現する
- "There is 〜" という形で、「〜がある」と表現する
- "a lot of 〜" という形で「〜がたくさん」と表現する
- "a little 〜" で「少しの〜」と表現する
- "some 〜" で「いくらかの〜」と表現する
- 冠詞の a や語尾の s は付けない。

「数えられる」とは、「始めと終わりがあるもの」ともいえる。つまり、どこからどこまでその「もの」であるか、はっきりしているとき、その「もの」は数えられる。

どこから、どこまでが「りんご」でどこからが背景かがわかる⇒1つのりんご、と数える。

「情報」→どこからどこまでが「情報」なのかはあいまい ⇒ ✗ a information / informations

「机＝ a desk」は数えられる（どこからどこまでが机かがわかる）がその材料である「木材＝ wood」は数えない。

（「木＝ tree」は数えられる）

形のないもの、小さすぎて形がないように見えるもの、形がひとつに決まっていないもの、色々なものの集合であるためにひとつの形ではないものは、数えられません。

Unit 5 There is / There are / It is / They are
「ある」「いる」の表現と It is / They are との違い

何かがある、いる、誰かがいる、を表現したい時には **There is 〜 / There are 〜**という表現を使います。あるもの、いるものが単数形もしくは数えられない名詞（液体など）の場合は There is 〜, 数えられる複数形のものの場合は There are 〜になります。

★ **They are 〜（それら・彼らは〜です）と間違えやすいので注意しましょう。**
　　例) **They** are students. 彼らは学生（たち）**です。**
　　　　There are students. 学生（たち）**がいます。**

★ There is / There are は新しい存在の情報を示します。したがって、There is / There are と一緒に所有格(my/his/her/their など) や the は通常使えません。

　　また、時制に応じて Be 動詞を変化させます。例えば、
　　・過去形（〜がいた、〜があった）なら There **was** 〜 / There **were** 〜,
　　・現在完了形（〜がこれまでずっとある、いる）なら、There **has been** 〜 / There **have been** 〜
　　・過去完了形（〜がそれまであった、いた）なら There **had been** 〜になります。（単数複数共通）

★ There is / There are の there には 「**そこに」という意味は含まれません。**場所を示したい時は文頭や文末に加えます。例えば：
　　There is a chair **there**. 「そこに椅子が一脚**あります」**
　　There are ten chairs in the classroom. 「教室には椅子が 10 脚あります」
　　There were a lot of people at the concert. 「コンサート（会場）には大勢の人がいました」
　　There is some apple juice in the fridge. 「冷蔵庫にはりんごジュースが入っています」
　　In Tokyo, there are many good restaurants. 「東京には多くの良いレストランがあります」

★ 「うちは〜人家族です」と言いたい場合、英語では「家族というユニット（グループ）の中に〜人の人がいる」という考え方をするため、There are 〜 を使って表現します。
　　例えば「私は四人家族です」と言いたい場合は **There are 4 people in my family.** といいます。そしてその四人が**どのような人々かについては、They are 〜** を使います。
　　例) "There are four people in my family. They are my father, my mother, my older sister, and me."

★ there is 〜 / there are 〜はいまそこに存在する（物理的にそこにある、いる、抽象概念の場合でもそこにそれが存在する）という意味を持ちます。したがって、日本語で「いる」「ある」と表現する場合でも「所有」を表すときには there is / there are ではなく have をつかって表現するので注意。例:「私には兄弟がいる」（所有）
　　→ I have a brother.
　　「うちには犬がいます」（所有）→ We have a dog.
　　「通りには犬がいます」（存在）→ There is a dog in the street.

★ 「〜には〜はいますか」「〜には〜はありますか」という疑問文をつくる場合は（所有以外）Be 動詞を there の前にして文頭を大文字にし、any や数を表す語句を用います。「〜がない」という否定文の場合は Be 動詞に not をつけ、名詞の前に any をおきます。

「その部屋に椅子はありますか」Are there any chairs in that room?「人はたくさんいましたか」Were there a lot of people?「そこには本はありませんでした」There aren't any books there.

完了形の場合は have だけを前にだします：「間違いがあったのですか？」Has there been a mistake? / Is there a mistake?

It is 〜 / They are 〜：「それは〜だ、それら・彼らは〜だ」の表現

「それは〜だ」「それら・彼らは〜だ」と言いたい場合は It is 〜 / They are 〜を使います。単数形のものには It is 〜複数形のものには They are を使います。

It is / They are には名詞、もしくは形容詞が続きます。名詞の前に形容詞がつくこともあります。

例）It is a textbook.　それは教科書です。

　　It is good.　それはよい・それはおいしい

　　It is a good textbook.　それはよい教科書です。

　　They are textbooks.

　　They are good.

　　They are good textbooks.

　　They are Japanese.　彼らは日本人です。

　　They are Japanese companies.　それらは日本の会社です。

名詞で終わる場合、通常冠詞（a/an/the）が必要です。数えられるもので一つなら a, 数えられる 1 つのもので母音で始まる名詞には an、「その〜」と特定できるものには the がつきます。数えられるもので複数の場合は名詞に s や es をつけて複数形にして、they are に続けます。

例）It is the book we use for our English class this year.　これが英語の授業で使う教科書です。

　　It is an apple, not an orange.　これはりんごだよ、オレンジじゃないよ。

　　They are Japanese books.　それらは日本の本です。

　　時制が変化した場合は Be 動詞の部分を変化させましょう。

　　It is 〜 → It was 〜, It has been 〜, It had been 〜

　　They are → They were 〜, They have been 〜, They had been 〜

　　疑問文を作る時は、それぞれ動詞を前にだします：Is it 〜 / Are they 〜？

　　Is it a good book? Are they nice? Are they Japanese?

Unit 6 Cardinal & Ordinal Numbers
数

1 one 2 two 3 three 4 four 5 five 6 six 7 seven 8 eight 9 nine 10 ten 11 eleven 12 twelve

[13 ～ 19：--teen]

13 thirteen 14 fourteen 15 fifteen 16 sixteen 17 seventeen 18 eighteen 19 nineteen

[20, 30, 40, 50, 60,70, 80, 90：--ty]

20 twenty 30 thirty 40 forty 50 fifty 60 sixty 70 seventy 80 eighty 90 ninety

[21 ～ 29 twenty--]

21 twenty-one 22 twenty-two 23 twenty-three 24 twenty-four
25 twenty-five 26 twenty-six 27 twenty-seven 28 twenty-eight 29 twenty-nine

31-39 thirty--
41-49 forty--
51-59 fifty--
61-69 sixty--
71-79 seventy--
81-89 eighty--
91-99 ninety--

英語の数字の読み方

英語は0が3つで単位が上がっていきます：

1 （一） one
10 （十） ten
100 （百） one hundred
1,000 （千） one thousand
10,000 （一万） ten thousand
100,000 （十万） one hundred thousand
1,000,000 （百万） one million
10,000,000 （千万） ten million
100,000,000 （一億） one hundred million
1,000,000,000 （十億） one billion
10,000,000,000 （百億） ten billion
100,000,000,000 （千億） one hundred billion
1,000,000,000,000 （一兆） one trillion

```
100 の位              ＝ 数＋ hundred ... one hundred, two hundred, three hundred ...
1000 の位             ＝ 数＋ thousand ... one thousand, two thousand, three thousand ...
10,000        ＝ 1 万      ＝ 10 と千      ＝ ten + thousand
100,000       ＝ 10 万     ＝ 100 と千     ＝ one hundred + thousand
1,000,000     ＝ 100 万    ＝ one million
10,000,000    ＝ 1000 万   ＝ 10 と million
100,000,000   ＝ 1 億      ＝ 100 と million
1,000,000,000 ＝ 10 億     ＝ one billion
10,000,000,000 ＝ 100 億    ＝ 10 と billion
100,000,000,000 ＝ 1000 億   ＝ 100 と billion
1,000,000,000,000 ＝ 1 兆    ＝ one trillion
```

序数（一番目、二番目…）の読み方

1 ～ 3 まで

> 1st first　2nd second　3rd third

4 からは ⇒ -th をつける：

> 4th fourth　5th fifth　6th sixth　7th seventh　8th eighth　9th ninth　10th tenth
> 11th eleventh　12th twelfth

13 からは ⇒ -teenth

> 13th thirteenth　14th fourteenth　15th fifteenth　16th sixteenth　17th seventeenth
> 18th eighteenth　19th nineteenth

20、30、40 などの の -ty は -ti にかえて

> 20 twenty → 20th twentieth

21 からは ⇒ twenty ＋

> 21st twenty-first　22nd twenty-second　23rd　twenty-third　24th twenty-fourth
> 31st thirty-first　42nd forty-second　53rd fifty-third　64th sixty-fourth

100 以上も同様

> 100th (one) hundredth　　101st (one) hundred-first　　102nd (one) hundred-second
> 103rd (one) hundred-third　　104th (one) hundred-fourth

西暦の表現方法

～ 1990 年代まで：二つの部分に分けて数えます：1991 → 19 と 91　nineteen / ninety-one

2000 ～ ：現在のところ二つの数え方があります：2019　two thousand nineteen

twenty nineteen

Unit 7 Past Tense
過去形

単純過去形

① 行為が過去のある明確な時点に始まり、そして終わったということを表すために使われます。

例）"I visited a museum yesterday."
→「昨日」という特定の時点で、「博物館を訪れ、その行為を終えた」ことを示す。

例）"Did you have dinner?"
→「いつ」とは書かれていないが、過去のある時点で「食べた」かどうかをきいている。

☆連続した動作（「～して、～して、～した」というような表現）でも過去形を繰り返し使います。

例）I **added** some sugar, **poured** some milk, and **mixed** it with a spoon.

例）I **visited** a museum, **saw** some great drawings, and **had** some tea.

② 過去における持続（「～していた」）を表します。期間をあらわす表現（～年間、～時間など）と一緒に用いることが多いです。

例）I **lived** in the U.S.A. **for 3 years**. 「３年間アメリカに住んでいました」

例）We **studied** all day. 「私たちは一日中勉強していました」

例）We **chatted** on the phone **for one hour**. 「１時間も電話でおしゃべりをしていました」

③「昔は～した・だった」という表現として用いられます。（used to ～と同様の意味を持つ）

例）I **played** baseball when I was a child. 「子供の時、はよく野球をしました」

例）He **didn't like** carrots before. 「彼は昔は人参が好きではありませんでした」

例）She **was** very quiet as a student, but now she is very cheerful as a teacher.
「彼女は学生としては静かな方だったが、教員になった今はすごく朗らかだ」

一般動詞は以下のパターンで変化します：

Regular verbs（規則動詞）を過去形にするには、現在形に、−ed または −d を語尾に付けます。

> walk（現在）−walked（過去）−walked（過去分詞）, move-moved-moved, start-started-started,
> stay-stayed-stayed, study-studied-studied

規則動詞・過去形の発音

- p, f, k, s, sh, ch, th で終わる語の過去形は ed がついても "t" の音で発音します
  （「トゥッ」と早く言ってみてください。）　例）walked ウォークトゥッ
- 早く言ってみてください。）例）moved モーヴドゥ
- もし動詞が t か d で終わる語の場合、過去形の発音は ed がついて "id" となります。
  （「イドゥ」と短くいう感じです）　例）started「スターティイドゥ」

不規則動詞では、以下のどれかのパターンになります。

1. sing-sang（i-a）i が a に変わるパターン
2. fly-flew（"ew" ending）ew で終わる形になるパターン
3. take-took（"ook" ending）ook で終わる形になるパターン
4. make-made（past tense ends with "d" sound）d の音になるパターン
5. buy-bought（"aught/ought" ending）aught や ought になるパターン
6. sleep-slept（"t" ending）t で終わるパターン
7. cut-cut（no changes）綴りに変化がないパターン　＊発音だけが変わるものもあります。
   例）read-read-read
8. Other verbs change in specific ways and must be memorized: be, see, go, do, come, run, etc.
   他にも特別な形をとるために、覚えてしまう方が早いものもあります→ be, see, go, do, come など。

   ☆多くの動詞が不規則変化します。スペルが変わるので、基本的な単語は覚えてしまいましょう。

- 一般動詞の過去形を使って否定文や疑問文を作るには、did を用います。動詞は原形に戻します。疑問文の場合は文頭に置いて大文字で始めます。否定文の場合は did not (didn't) を動詞の原形の前に置きます。
  Did you **go** to the party last night?「昨晩はパーティに行ったの？」
  I **didn't go** to the party last night.「昨晩はパーティに行きませんでした。」

Unit 8 Time
時間の表現

時間の言い方

英語で時間を表現するには：

　　① 日本語と同じように、時間（hours）を先に言う
　　②「分」の部分から先に言う

　　　　　　　　　　　　　　　　　　　　　　　　　　　の2つの言い方があります。

日常的によく用いられるのが、②の「分」を先に言うものです。①の言い方は、よりフォーマルなものになります。
以下の例で見てみましょう。

① 時間を先にいう場合（正式）	②「分」を先にいう場合（会話調）
1:05 = one oh five	five after one/five past one
1:10 = one ten	ten after one/ten past one
1:15 = one fifteen	a quarter after one/a quarter past one
1:30 = one thirty	half past one
1:35 = one thirty-five	twenty-five to two
1:45 = one forty-five	a quarter to two

　　15分過ぎには、fifteen / a quarter after / a quarter past の4つ
　　45分過ぎには、forty-five / a quarter to の2つ
　　30分過ぎには、thirty / half past の2つ
　の言い方があります

時間の聞き方

"What's the time?", "What time is it?" または "Do you have the time?" と聞きます。
時間を答えるには it's を使います。誰かに時間を聞かれたら以下のように答えましょう。
　　"**It's** ten after/past four." または "**It's** a quarter to five."

何かを何時に行うか、何が何時に起こるか、についての質問には、at を使って答えます。
　　"I have dinner **at** half past seven." OR "My first class starts **at** nine o'clock."

※ 24時間表記を用いた時間表現は、米軍内など軍事的な状況においてのみ使われます。一般的な会話では a.m./
　p.m. を使います。例）"It's 1:00 p.m."（Not 13:00）

時間の長さ（～分、～時間など）を表現するには、for を用います。
　　I was there **for** one hour.「そこには1時間いました。」

期間（～の間に）を表現するには、during を用います。
　　I went to Kyoto **during** summer vacation.「夏休みの間、京都に行きました。」

Unit 9 Present Perfect
現在完了形

現在完了形は、**過去に何が起きたのか、ではなく、過去に開始された行為が、現在と関わっているとき**、以下の3つを示すときに、have(has) ＋過去分詞を用いて表します。以下に、過去形との違いを確認しながら見ていきましょう。

3つの用法
・過去に開始された行為がどう今に至っているか（すでに〜した、まだ〜していない）
・過去の行為を経験として表現すること（〜したことがある）
・過去に始めた行為が今も続いていること（ずっと〜している）

① 結果用法・完了用法 「どうなったか」ではなく「どうなって今に至っているか」
例） I have already finished my homework. 宿題はすでに終えた（終えている状態に今ある）
　　※過去形の I finished my homework. は、どこかの時点で宿題を終えた、という事実だけを表す。
例） She has bought a new computer. 新しいコンピュータを買った（そして今それを所有している）
　　※過去形の She bought a new computer だと「新しいコンピュータを買った」ということのみを表す。

② 経験用法 過去に何をしたことがあるか（何をしたか、ではなく、何を「したことがある」か）
例） I have eaten Turkish food before. トルコ料理を食べたことがある。
　　※過去形の I ate Turkish food yesterday などにすると、昨日「トルコ料理を食べた」ということのみを表す。
例） I have never been to London. ロンドンには行ったことがない。
　　※過去形の I didn't go to London last year. →昨年という時点で、ロンドンに「行かなかった」ということのみを表す

③ 継続用法 過去に始まった行為等が、現在まで継続している
例） I have lived in Japan for 30 years. 日本に住んで30年になります。（30年前に日本に住み始めて、30年間日本に「住む」ことを継続している。）
　　※過去形 I lived in Japan when I was a child →子供のころという時点で、日本に住んでいた、ということのみを表す。

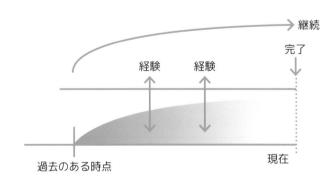

Unit 10 Auxiliary Verbs
助動詞

助動詞とは、文字通り、**文章の中で動詞を助けるもの**です。ここでいう「助ける」とは、**動詞だけでは、文章の意味や役割を完結できない場合**に用いられる、ということになります。
例えば「走る」という動詞があった場合、「走るつもり」「走ってきた」「走ることができる」「走ることができるかもしれない」という意味にするためには、助動詞が必要です。

これを踏まえ、助動詞は大きく二つに分けられます。
① 疑問文・否定文・完了形・受動態などに使うもの（do / have / be）
② 動詞の原形の前において話し手の心理を動詞の意味に加えるもの
　（will / can / may / must / should / might など）

それでは、それぞれの助動詞がどのように動詞を助けるのか見ていきましょう。

第①グループ

do – 動詞を疑問形・否定形にする役割
　　「〜する」 ➡ 「〜しますか」「〜しない」
have – 動詞を完了形にする役割
　　「〜する」 ➡ 「〜してきたところ」「〜したことがある」「ずっと〜している」
be – 動詞を受動態にする役割
　　「〜する」 ➡ 「〜される」

第②グループ

will – 動詞を未来形にする役割と動詞に意志を加える役割
　　「〜する」 ➡ 「〜する（予定）」「〜するつもり」
can – 動詞に能力・可能性・許可の意味を加える役割
　　「〜する」 ➡ 「〜できる」「〜しうる」「〜していい」
may – 動詞に推測・許可・祈願の意味を加える役割
　　「〜する」 ➡ 「〜するかもしれない」「〜してもよい」「〜しますように」
might – 動詞に推測の意味を加える役割（may よりも弱い推測）
　　「〜する」 ➡ 「〜するかもしれない」
have to/must – 動詞に義務・禁止・強い推奨・強い確信の意味を加える役割
　　「〜する」 ➡ 「〜しなければならない」「絶対〜したほうがいい」「〜する違いない」
should – 動詞に義務・確信の意味を加える
　　「〜する」 ➡ 「〜すべき」「〜するはず」
shall – 動詞に勧誘や申し出の意味を加える役割
　　「〜する」 ➡ 「〜しましょう（か）」
would – 動詞に過去の時点での未来・意志・過去の習慣の意味を加える役割
　　「〜する」 ➡ 「よく〜した」
could– 動詞に過去の時点での能力、現時点での婉曲や想像の意味を加える役割
　　「〜する」 ➡ 「〜することができた」「〜することもできるだろう」「〜することもありうる」
　第２グループ助動詞の位置は、平叙文では常に動詞のすぐ前です。そして、動詞は必ず原形にします。
　　　例）You can sing.

Unit 11 Future Tense
未来形

英語で未来を表現するには、主に３つの表現方法があります。以下で確認しましょう。

1. **現在形**（Simple present）スケジュールや時刻表などに使います。

   What time **does** the next train **leave**?「次の電車は何時発？」

   The next bus **doesn't leave** until 6 p.m. tonight.「次のバスは今夜 6 時までありません」

   Class **starts** at 8:30 tomorrow morning.「授業は明日朝 8 時半に始まります」

   We **check in** after we arrive at the hotel.「ホテルについてからチェックインします」

2. **現在進行形**（Present continuous (be + ing)）確定している予定、わかっている予定に使います

   I'm **finishing** my report tonight.「今夜レポートを終わらせます」

   They**'re coming** over to my place after school「彼らは今日の放課後、私のうちにきます」

   She**'s leaving** for New York on Monday.「彼女は月曜日にニューヨークに発ちます」

   I'm **not inviting** her to the party.「彼女は今度のパーティにはよばないわ」

3. **Be going to (do)**   計画済みのこと、する（しない）つもり、起きる（起きない）だろうことに使います。

   We**'re going to work** outside this weekend.「この週末、我々は外仕事をする予定にしているんだ」

   I'm **going to visit** Paris after I graduate.「卒業したら、パリにいくつもり」

   It looks like it**'s going to rain** this afternoon.「今日の午後には雨がふる感じだね」

   He**'s going to finish** his report tomorrow.「彼は明日レポートを終わらせる予定です」

   I'm **not going to see** him again.「もう彼に会うつもりはないわ」

4. **Will (do)/won't (will not) do**   その場で決めたことや意志未来に使います。

   (Ordering in a restaurant): I**'ll have** the mixed pizza and oolong tea, please.
   (レストランで注文している時)「ミックスピザと烏龍茶をいただきます」

   Japan **will win** the World Cup next time for sure.「日本は次の W 杯では絶対勝つね」

   I **will show** you where to find everything you need.「必要なものがどこにあるか案内しますね」

   Dan **won't** see him again.「ダンはもう彼には会わないって」

★ be going to と will の使い分け

will には名詞では「意志」「遺書」の意味があります。したがって、will には「〜する意志がある、〜しない意志がある」という意味合いが強くなります。つまり「予定」というよりも、自分がなにかを「する」つもり、という意志の意味合いが強くなるということです。be going to は、すでに決めたことについて言うときに使います。つまり、自分が何かをする「つもり」でいるという意味合いが強くなります。以下の例で違いを見てみましょう。

   A: Do you know Mark is in the hospital?

   B: Really? I didn't know that. I **will** go and visit him in the hospital this evening.

   ....

   A: Do you know Mark is in the hospital?

   B. Yes, I know. I **am going to** visit him in the hospital this evening.

※ "shall" について

アメリカ英語では、shall を未来時制として用いる（例：I shall go tomorrow.「明日行きます」など）は、旧式であまり用いられません。アメリカ英語で shall は「〜しましょうか」と申し出をするときにのみ、使います。ただし、イギリス英語では、未来時制としての shall は現在でもよく使われます。

Unit 12 Prepositions
前置詞

前置詞（propositions）とは、**名詞（または名詞の働きをする語）の前**において、その名詞に、**時や場所等の意味を補って、他の語とその名詞がどのような関係であるか**を示すものです。

日本語にはない品詞ですが、**日本語の助詞「で」「に」「の」「へ」「から」「まで」「と」などに近い働き**をします。

例えば "I go to school." の前置詞 "to" は「school」という名詞に「〜に」（または「〜へ」）という意味を補うことで、「I go」という他の言葉と「school」という名詞がどのような関係を表すか、ということを示しています。

前置詞には多くの種類がありますが、最もよく使われるのは、**of, in, to, for, on, with, at, by, from** です。下記には、どう訳されることが多いかを示していますが、前置詞を理解するポイントは、和訳でとらえるのではなく、具体的なイメージで捉えることが大切です。

まずはよく使われる前置詞のイメージについて確認しましょう。

at のイメージ

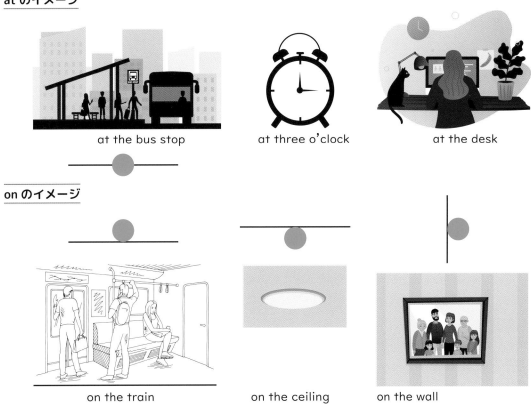

at the bus stop　　　at three o'clock　　　at the desk

on のイメージ

on the train　　　on the ceiling　　　on the wall

in のイメージ

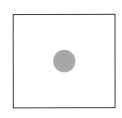

in a room

次に、「時」と「場所」に関する基本的な前置詞（おもに Unit で扱ったもの）についてみていきます。具体的な用法とより抽象的な用法があります。その共通点についても考えてみましょう。

「時」に関するもの

➡ 年月、日時などを示す前置詞例

「〜に」と訳すことが多いですが、どのような名詞が後に来るかによって、使うものが異なります。

at：時刻や、ある特定の期間 といった「時の一点」を表します。

☆ 指が差せるようなピンポイント感のある前置詞です。

at five o'clock 五時に　　**at** noon 正午に　　**at** night 夜に　　**at** New Year's 年末年始に

at Christmas クリスマスの時期に

on：曜日や日付など特定の日を表します。

on Monday 月曜日に　　**on** Sundays 毎週日曜日に　　**on** December 5th 12 月 5 日に

on your birthday あなたの誕生日に　　**on** the evening of September 9th 9 月 9 日の夜に

in：月、四季、年、世紀など長い単位に用います。

in April 四月に　　**in** summer 夏に　　**in** 2020 ２０２０年に　　**in** the 21st Century ２１世紀に

➡ 時の起点を示す前置詞例

after：ある時点以降について用います。

I will be free **after** 6 o'clock.　　六時以降はひまです。

➡ 時の終点を示す前置詞例

before：「〜の前に」という意味を表します

I went to run **before** breakfast this morning.　　今朝、朝食の前に走りに行った。

「場所」に関するもの

at：「〜に（いる）」「〜で（待つ）」などと訳されるもの。場所を広がりのある空間ではなく、点としてとらえる時に用いる。例えば、「学校にいる」といいたいときは、必ずしも学校という建物の「中」にいる、と言いたいわけではなく、学校を点としての場所ととらえて、学校という場所にいるという意味なので、I'm at school といいます。（反対に学校の建物の中にいる、ときは I'm in the school building となります）

"Where are you? I just arrived **at** the station."「どこにいる？ 駅に着いたところだよ」

I feel **at** home.「家にいるみたいだ」（※家の中という意味ではなく、家という場所にいるようだという意味）

Please look **at** me.「私をみて」

in：「〜の中にいる」という意味。日本語で「中」という訳にならなくても、広がりを持った空間のどこかにいるという意味の場合は in を使います。

I'm **in** France right now.「今フランスにいます」（※フランスという国境内のどこかにいるので in）

"I'm at the station now" "OK, I will be there soon. Are you **in** the station or outside?"

「駅にいます」「わかりました。もうすぐつきます。駅の中にいますか？ それとも外？」

That actor starred **in** many movies.「あの俳優はたくさんの映画にでていましたね」

on：「上に」と訳されることが多いですが、「上」というよりも、接触を表します。したがって、壁に貼ってあるもの、天井にあるものにも用います。また、上から何かを見下ろす、と言う場合にも、視線が何かと接触していると考えるため on を用います。

The time table is **on** the wall.「時刻表は壁にはってあります。」

There are a lot of lights **on** the hotel ceiling.「そのホテルの天井にはたくさんの照明がついていた」

She was looking down **on** the street from her window.「彼女は部屋の窓から、通りを見下ろしていた」

Don't look down **on** me.「軽蔑しないでよ」（※自分を見下ろす→軽蔑する、という表現）

Project English   [B-936]
An Activity-based Guide to Everyday Conversation and Basic Grammar
アクティブに学ぶ英語コミュニケーション

| 1 刷 | 2022 年 2 月 17 日 |
| 2 刷 | 2023 年 3 月 31 日 |

| 著　者 | 師岡　ヴィヴィアン　　Vivian Morooka |
| | 足立　綾　　　　　　Aya Adachi |

発行者　南雲　一範　Kazunori Nagumo
発行所　株式会社　南雲堂
　　　　〒162-0801　東京都新宿区山吹町361
　　　　NAN'UN-DO Co., Ltd.
　　　　361 Yamabuki-cho, Shinjuku-ku, Tokyo 162-0801, Japan
　　　　振替口座：00160-0-46863
　　　　TEL:　03-3268-2311（営業部：学校関係）
　　　　　　　03-3268-2384（営業部：書店関係）
　　　　　　　03-3268-2387（編集部）
　　　　FAX:　03-3269-2486

編集者	加藤　敦
組　版	柴崎　利恵
装　丁	銀月堂　（イラスト：ヨシオカ　ユリ）
イラスト	ヨシオカ　ユリ（扉・p12-13・各ユニット冒頭・p94-95）
検　印　省　略	
コード	ISBN978-4-523-17936-8　　　　　　　　C0082

Printed in Japan

E-mail : nanundo@post.email.ne.jp
URL : https://www.nanun-do.co.jp/